Serving Students Who Are Homeless

Serving Students Who Are Homeless

A Resource Guide for Schools, Districts, Educational Leaders, and Community Partners

SECOND EDITION

Ronald E. Hallett, Ann M. Aviles, and Linda Skrla

Foreword by Zach Stumbo

Published by Teachers College Press,® 1234 Amsterdam Avenue, New York, NY 10027

Front cover illustration by Barks Japan / iStock by Getty Images.

Library of Congress Cataloging-in-Publication Data is available at loc.gov

ISBN 978-0-8077-8744-1 (paper)
ISBN 978-0-8077-8745-8 (hardcover)
ISBN 978-0-8077-8327-6 (ebook)

Printed on acid-free paper
Manufactured in the United States of America

Contents

Foreword to the First Edition

The book you are about to read by Dr. Ronald E. Hallett and Dr. Linda Skrla provides an excellent overview of homelessness, the possible reasons that families and students may find themselves in this predicament, and the effect it may have on children and their academic success.

It offers an in-depth look into the influence of policy, school leadership, and the professional development provided for support counselors, teachers, and administrators on how they address the needs of students within their district who are facing homelessness. Community outreach, research identification, and trauma-informed care practices are just a few of the topics addressed that have intrinsic value to ensure the academic success of these students.

I met Dr. Ronald Hallett when I was the homeless liaison for the Los Angeles Unified School District. The plight of homeless children has been at the core of his work since he began his career as a teacher. Having conducted research on children experiencing homelessness in Los Angeles, his work sheds light on the difficulties these students deal with in order to remain connected to school, graduate, and pursue their dreams.

His partner in this book, Dr. Linda Skrla, also began her work in schools as a teacher and an administrator. As time progressed, she began to focus on educational equity issues in school leadership. The pairing of their work, along with the depth and breadth of their expertise, has created a unique overview of homelessness and provides credible insight into this issue and the ways in which we can support children who are struggling with this problem.

Years of research reveal that the impact of homelessness on education can be devastating: Many students facing homelessness do not finish high school or go on to any postsecondary program, thus continuing the cycle of poverty. Stability in such unstable times is paramount to the child's academic success; schools can be a source of strength and provide valuable resources for families and children. This book will enable readers to more fully understand the issues at play; assist practitioners, advocates, and administrators to create or revise current policy and practice; and encourage the utilization of various strategies in order to support these students as they work to meet their full academic potential.

As the Los Angeles County Office of Education Homeless consultant, I support the efforts of the homeless liaisons designated within the 80 school districts and more than 170 charter schools across Los Angeles County who have identified nearly 55,000 homeless students, infants through 12th grade, in their schools and local community. I have worked in this realm for more than a decade and, sadly, the numbers of homeless families and children continue to rise. The information and strategies identified within the pages of this book will prove to be an invaluable resource to the work of counselors, school personnel, teachers, administrators, and advocates for homeless students. This book will be a welcome addition to your library.

—Melissa Schoonmaker
Los Angeles County Office of Education

Foreword to the Second Edition

Dr. Ronald E. Hallett and Dr. Linda Skrla authored the first edition of this book, which provided a research-based look into the lived experiences of students and families experiencing homelessness. This edition, with the additional insights of Dr. Ann M. Aviles, serves as an updated comprehensive introduction to the systems that impact housing insecurity and how these systems often affect students experiencing homelessness.

The book is organized into three overarching sections. The first third discusses the various systems impacting unhoused students. The second section offers a solution-focused discussion on ensuring educational access for students who experience homelessness. The final section inspires readers to aim for more than mere compliance with local, state, and federal laws by advocating for innovative program designs that support students' transitions beyond high school.

I first learned of Dr. Hallett while researching professional development tools for local homeless liaisons across my home state. I selected the first edition of this book because of its organizational strengths. Each section is organized into chapters and subchapters that connect concepts and introduce new ideas, making it well suited for a book study. Additionally, I chose this text based on my lived experience as a former homeless youth and my professional experience as a teacher, teacher educator, and educational policy consultant. After selecting the book, I met Dr. Hallett when I invited him to be a keynote speaker at an annual professional development event attended by nearly 200 school professionals. His speech was as powerful and inspiring as this text.

This book weaves together research findings, best practices, thoughtful reflections, and students' needs into one resource. I have found that professionals and volunteers working with students experiencing homelessness have varied levels of preparation, leading to inconsistencies in the support delivered. The book provides a holistic view of educating homeless students in a manageable and approachable manner. As such, it is recommended reading for state coordinators and local homeless liaisons under the McKinney-Vento Act, school professionals, health care providers, and other community stakeholders. Readers will be encouraged to prioritize the identification of students experiencing homelessness. Once identified, students will benefit from the reader's advocacy for school stability, referrals to supportive agencies, and the removal of barriers caused by homelessness.

My personal experience with housing insecurity as a child was extensive. In the early days of the McKinney-Vento Act, I lived in a doubled-up situation with my mother and grandmother following my parents' divorce. As an elementary and middle school child, I experienced living in substandard conditions that included infestations and occasional interruptions in utility services. One week after I turned 18, during my junior year of high school, I was no longer welcome to live at home. I finished high school surfing from couch to couch until college. Nevertheless, I became the first member of my family to graduate from college. I later completed a master's in teacher leadership and a PhD in teacher education.

My story was only possible because of the support I received to finish high school and attend college. I am confident that readers of this book will be prepared to support today's students experiencing homelessness. As school districts continue to combat learning loss, rising chronic absenteeism, and concerning academic indicators, it will be crucial to have a unified vision of support. I cannot recommend a better starting point than this text.

—Zach Stumbo
Homeless Education Coordinator
Division of School and Program Improvement
Kentucky Department of Education

CHAPTER 1

Introduction

"Most people think that we are bad kids," said Benjamin, a 15-year-old, who has lived in Skid Row for five years. "We're not; we just like anyone else."

The demographic context of public schools in the United States has changed over the past few decades. Low-income students now represent the majority of students served in public schools (Southern Education Foundation, 2015). Persistent economic challenges and a growing income divide have resulted in fewer households earning enough to achieve economic stability. Families who are categorized as "the working poor" often live paycheck to paycheck, which puts them constantly on the edge of an economic crisis. How teachers, administrators, community leaders, and policymakers approach their work should reflect the changing realities of students and families.

A growing subpopulation of students remains invisible—students experiencing homelessness and housing insecurity. Students from these families often hide to avoid social shame and fear the consequences of being exposed. Even when these young people and their families emerge from the shadows, figuring out how to provide educational support can seem overwhelming for schools, districts, and community leaders. To further complicate the issue, these students were unseen by district, state, and federal tracking systems for many years, which made assessing their performance and addressing their needs difficult to accomplish. However, federal mandates within the Every Student Succeeds Act [ESSA] of 2015 now require reporting on the academic outcomes of students experiencing homelessness. Engaging with data at the local, state, and national levels can help to illuminate that size and scope of youth and family homelessness, which gives educators and policymakers a base to build upon as they collaboratively explore effective supports and interventions.

Students who are homeless endure real challenges. Benjamin's comment above demonstrates several of the concepts that serve as the foundations for this book. Students experiencing homelessness want to engage in the educational system; however, the trauma and shame their circumstances produce limit their ability to do so. These students' residential experiences impact their ability to fully access school. Often, they are labeled as disruptive or truant. While their external behaviors may seem to justify such identifiers, digging deeper into their lived experiences often reveals traumatic incidents that warrant consideration when creating a supportive educational context where these students can thrive. These young people and their families may not know they are entitled to educational support, and the school may be unaware that state and federal aid may be available to implement services to support these students.

An important note about terminology is warranted. As explained in Chapter 3, the federal government employs an inclusive definition of homelessness in the educational context. While the common image of homelessness may be of someone living on the street or in a shelter, students considered homeless are far more likely to live in other unstable and precarious spaces. If a school enrolls no students who live on the street or in shelters, school administrators may think "homelessness" does not apply to its population. However, such a school may have large numbers of students living in hotels, motels, or doubled-up residences (homes or apartments designed for a single family that house two or more family units). In rural communities, a school district may have several families living in barns, tents, or vehicles in areas that may be out of sight. These more hidden forms of homelessness account for a large proportion of students experiencing homelessness.

Two issues undergird the ideas presented in this book. First, homelessness no longer exists only at the fringes of society. The persistent economic conditions within the United States have led to a growing subpopulation of students experiencing homelessness within schools and districts across the nation. Second, finding ways to adequately serve students experiencing homelessness is an educational access issue. As discussed in Chapter 2, educators play a key role in supporting these students' success. We explore these ideas in greater depth throughout the book but provide a brief introduction to serve as a foundation.

MAGNITUDE OF STUDENT HOMELESSNESS

Many people underestimate how many young people experience homelessness in the United States. While getting an exact count is difficult, current estimates suggest the following:

- 1.2 million students in PK–12 experience homelessness each year—or approximately 1 in every 40 students (Endres & Cidade, 2015; National Center for Homeless Education, 2023).
- 1.2 to 1.45 million children under the age of 6 experience homelessness each year—or 1 in every 16 individuals within this age group (National Center on Early Childhood Health and Wellness, 2024; SchoolHouse Connection, 2020).

- The rate of homelessness among PK–12 students increased by 79% between the 2004–2005 and 2021–2022 academic years (National Center for Homeless Education, 2023).
- 10.5 million students attend high-poverty schools (National Center for Education Statistics, 2024).
- 15% of children under the age of 18 live below the poverty rate—with six states having rates over 21% (Benson, 2023; U.S. Census Bureau, 2021).
- 68% of students experiencing homelessness graduate from high school, which is 12% lower than their low-income peers who are stably housed and 18% lower than the overall student population (SchoolHouse Connection, 2025).

While information about students experiencing homelessness within PK–12 schools may seem shocking enough, they do not include the young people who are not enrolled or who have dropped out of the education system. Some estimates would suggest that nearly 2.5 million youth experience homelessness each year.

Many schools and districts now serve communities where over 10% of the student population lacks residential stability (Hallett et al., 2015a, 2015b). For example, in New York City schools, about 1 in 8 students experiences homelessness (Advocates for Children of New York, 2024). While this average may seem high, it disguises the more startling statistic that nine of the districts in New York City serve communities with approximately 20% of their students in homeless situations. Further, about 54% of students in these schools live doubled-up. Homelessness is not a fringe issue. As a superintendent in a rural community explained, he expects the students he serves to lack residential stability. This realization has changed how he thinks about the educational process and leads the school district. Achieving school- and district-level goals requires considering how to improve access to and success in PK–12 schools for students experiencing homelessness.

Serving students without residential stability requires rethinking what students need to be successful and how to implement support services within schools and districts. The impact of a single episode of homelessness on a young person extends beyond the struggle of enduring insufficient space for a period of time. Young people without residential stability experience trauma that negatively impacts their ability to fully engage with the educational process. Stability, predictability, and safety are taken from these children. Many students and families endure persistent residential instability that compounds the traumatic impact. These young people may experience homelessness throughout their entire time in school. In these cases, solutions require careful consideration of how policies and practices may need to shift in ways that encourage these students' educational success.

Some schools and communities have large numbers of young people in unstable residential situations, but the shame associated with this form of extreme poverty results in families and youth hiding their living situations from educators (Heerde et al., 2020; Tierney & Hallett, 2012). Students fear the social consequences of being identified as homeless. Christopher, a 19-year-old couch surfer (someone who sleeps on a series of friends' or acquaintances' couches or in their guest rooms), explained how he had a difficult time going to school because "the kids at the high school find out and they will tease you." Parents may fear having their children taken by social service agencies. Furthermore, educational leaders do not always understand the multiple forms of homelessness or how to identify students in different homeless situations. As a result, the magnitude of homelessness and residential instability in school and district settings can be overlooked.

Some readers may be keenly aware that this issue exists within their school and district. They may frequently interact with students and families who are trying to figure out how to remain engaged with school while meeting their basic needs. We appreciate that other readers may not perceive this issue as relevant within their community. There may not be homeless shelters near the school nor children living on the street. These forms of homelessness tend to be the most obvious but are not the most common for students. In the first section of this book, we provide both discussion about and illustration of the multiple forms of homelessness and residential instability. Most of these unstable situations may be invisible at first glance. Collection of new data or new approaches to data analysis may be needed to fully understand the extent of the issue within a local context. Many schools and districts in urban, rural, and suburban communities find that homelessness impacts a significant portion of their student body.

AN ISSUE OF ACCESS TO EDUCATION

Educators are accustomed to leveraging site and district data to inform practice. Data enable educators to explore if subgroups of students perform at rates similar to the overall population. Based upon continuous analysis of data, teachers, principals, and district leaders write reports that outline areas of growth and success as well as areas that call for improvement. Underperforming subgroups may receive additional programming and support. Educators receive professional development and engage in reflective evaluation of data to make decisions about how to encourage future achievement for these students. Schools and districts evaluate their successes based upon overall improvement and growth among subgroups. These data-informed approaches have the potential to make meaningful differences in improving student outcomes. But homelessness has not always been an issue schools and districts considered when evaluating student success. If it was not tracked—if data were not created and engaged with—educators could not have a clear picture of how these students performed or whether a specific intervention yielded positive results.

These students and their families live at the extreme end of the poverty continuum. They experience all the challenges of being low-income, but in more extreme ways that result in additional challenges. Thus, these students warrant concerted attention. As we discuss in Chapter 5, the revisions to the McKinney-Vento Homeless Assistance Act as part of the Every Student Succeeds Act (ESSA) now require tracking and accountability from schools, districts, and states. While the first step is to gain a clear picture of how many students within a school or district experience homelessness by gathering accurate data, the goal would be to explore how to leverage that information to make decisions about providing support at the classroom, school site, district and state levels that will bolster these students' educational success. Improving education access to students experiencing homelessness has the potential to significantly improve their chances of achieving future financial and residential stability. And improving the educational outcomes of these students will increase the overall educational outcomes for a school, district, or state.

STRUCTURE OF THE BOOK

This book explores how educational institutions can develop policies and practices that improve the educational outcomes of students experiencing homelessness. We avoid "Five Steps to Success" types of solutions. Complex social issues, like homelessness, can rarely be addressed with a simplistic approach. Rather, we share information that can be useful for educators as they interpret policy and develop programming within the local context. The ideas and suggestions presented are based upon research we have done in educational settings for over 2 decades as well as on our own experiences as educators. We also draw from the work of other researchers, policymakers, advocates, and educators who have dedicated their careers to improving educational opportunities for students experiencing homelessness. In the subsections that follow, we preview a few key aspects of the structure and how the book could be used to guide practice.

Student-First Language

We intentionally employ student-first language (e.g., "students experiencing homelessness" instead of "homeless students") for several reasons. First, many advocates of students and youth find that placing the *student* identity before the *marginalized* identity has significant implications for how educators view students as well as how students view themselves. Second, the categorization of any student as "homeless" is (hopefully) a temporary situation that will fade as students and families achieve housing stability. As such, giving language primacy to the more permanent and empowering identity—student—represents best practice. For many of these students, their lives revolve around their residential instability and related issues. At times, their student identity is threatened as basic needs take precedence. Educators can help these young people to feel more empowered as *students*. We strategically focus in this book on how to increase opportunities for these young people to develop as students. Relatedly, we encourage educators to use a similar approach when discussing families—for example, think and speak of "a family or parent experiencing homelessness" instead of "a homeless family."

Designed for Educators

This book is designed for educators interested in better understanding the issue of homelessness and the role they can play in helping these students fully access schooling. As we discuss in Chapter 2, we take a broad view of educators that includes teachers, staff, site administrators, community partners, and district and state leaders. We recognize that most schools exist within communities where local agencies, groups, and institutions provide support for young people and families—these educators can be important partners who teach students and families how to navigate the educational system and play a supportive role in improving student engagement. We developed the chapters to give practical and solutions-oriented guidance for educators in different roles. We recommend a collaborative approach that includes educators in different roles learning with each other and working together to implement solutions.

Continued Education Resources

To assist educators in thinking about how these complex issues can be addressed within the local context, we include resources and activities. Each chapter includes questions designed to help readers reflect on their work and consider how what they learned could be integrated into their practice. We also point to publicly available resources developed by researchers and practitioners. In addition, we encourage educators to consider developing a book club or professional learning community in order to explore ways to shift school, district, or state policies and practices. While individual educators can benefit from the book's contents and recommendations, a collaborative approach has the potential to broaden the positive impact.

PREVIEW OF THE BOOK

This book is divided into three parts. Part I focuses on exploring the issue of homelessness within the context of PK–12 education. We begin by discussing the multiple roles of educators and how each role is vital to the success of students. We show how doing this important work can impact educators. We then define and illustrate the diversity of residential situations that fall within the classification of *homeless*. In this revised edition, we present a new approach to supporting students experiencing homelessness: an *ecology of promise*. This approach affirms the importance of supporting the whole student, leveraging trauma-informed approaches, and reflecting upon and shifting the norms that guide interactions with students and colleagues. An ecology of promise perspective can be leveraged to review and revise policies and practices so as to support students more effectively.

Part II of the book begins with a discussion of the federal policies and guidelines that frame how schools, districts, and states support students experiencing homelessness. We highlight resources that assist educators in adjusting and aligning the policies and practices at the classroom, school site, district, and state levels. We also discuss the contexts of homelessness (e.g., unplanned mobility, connection to family, community-level disasters, and differences among rural, suburban, and urban communities) among students and families that frame how they navigate school. Of particular importance to educators, we explain the impact that homelessness and housing insecurity have on student outcomes.

Part III moves the conversation beyond educational access and toward academic success. We provide guidance related to adjusting school and district policies in ways that reflect the needs for students experiencing homelessness. We explore how educators and educational institutions can leverage partnerships with community members and institutions to more effectively provide support for students and their families. In addition to addressing the needs of students attending PK–12 schools, we encourage educators to consider how to support the postsecondary aspirations of students experiencing homelessness. In most cases, these students will need to earn a college degree or certificate to achieve long-term stability. We conclude with recommendations for continued learning and professional development focused on improving the academic outcomes of students experiencing homelessness.

Throughout this book, we draw from multiple sources (e.g., policy discussions, practitioner testimony, and research reports) to paint a picture of how homelessness and residential instability impact students and show why addressing this issue matters. Our goal is to provide resources and ideas for educators and administrators interested in adequately serving students experiencing homelessness, high rates of mobility, and other forms of residential instability.

The appendices include multiple activities designed for educators who want to move from learning toward implementing those ideas in their practice.

Building a Professional Learning Community

While this book can be read and used by individual educators, we also created activities at the end of each chapter that could be used within a *professional learning community* (PLC). A PLC provides the opportunity for a group of educators to learn with and from each other. In addition, PLCs create the space for educators within a school, community, district, or state to explore how to revise policies and practices at a broader level than is typically possible for an individual educator.

The structure of a PLC can differ depending upon the context and goals of the group. Educators could structure the PLC in different ways, including:

- A grade level within a school exploring how to improve their support of their students
- A school site integrating the content into the professional development for all educators
- A school leader creating a book club for educators who want to develop recommendations for improved practice at the site level
- A district unit or leadership team incorporating the book into their monthly meetings with the goal of reviewing and revising policies, practices, and support systems for students and families
- A district, county, or state coordinator including the book and activities within the training provided for homeless liaisons
- A community or state level organization that supports young people or families could engage with the activities to identify ways to partner more closely with schools and districts

PLCs could include cross-institutional members. For example, a school could invite individuals from local partner organizations, or a district may include leaders from community organizations to join a PLC with them. These cross-institutional PLCs create the space to explore how the institutions could collaborate to effectively support students and families experiencing homelessness. In cases where it may be difficult to have individuals outside of the school or district be a regular part of the PLC, educators could invite people to join specific conversations. For example, a school site could invite a group of parents to be part of a panel discussion about their experiences, or community organizations/groups could join a workshop exploring which resources are available in the local context and how to work collaboratively to fill gaps.

We suggest activities at the end of each chapter. However, PLCs may want to adjust these activities or develop new ones based upon their needs and goals. There are no "right" answers for each activity. The school, district, and state contexts frame what resources are available and what potential actions could be taken. Educators can assess potential shifts in policy and practice through the ecology of promise frame presented in Chapter 4.

CHAPTER CONCLUSION

As educators who have been significantly engaged with the intersection of homelessness and education for the past few decades, we recognize the importance of educators and educational institutions providing a pathway toward future stability for these students. Increasing educational access and success for students experiencing homelessness has the potential to change lives. We look forward to hearing more stories of schools and districts that identify and implement promising practices. The work that educators and educational leaders do is hard. And it matters.

One point that is worth emphasizing from the trauma-informed care literature: Student recovery is possible (Steele & Malchiodi, 2012). Homelessness, though a huge, complex, and frightening issue, does not have to be a signifier that individuals carry with them for life. Schools can, and do every day, serve as partners, safe harbors, solid structures, and educational lifelines that help students and families navigate seemingly desperate circumstances and move on to more stable and highly productive lives. Our own family histories include both homelessness and recovery, so lived experience underscores our commitment to this truth.

Guiding Questions

1. How many students and families within your school, community, district, and state experience homelessness? If institutions report different data, explore why this may be the case.
2. How do students and families within your local context experience homelessness and housing insecurity?
3. In what ways does your current role involve working with students and/or families experiencing homelessness?
4. What language does your school, community or district use to identify students and families experiencing homelessness? Are there opportunities to update terminology? If so, why might this be important?

PLC Activities

Activity 1: Creating Group Norms and Expectations

Educators reflect on their practice as well as on school, district, and/or state policies. For this group to be productive, it needs to be a space where people commit to learning with and from each other. Take time to establish group norms and expectations.

Activity 2: Getting to Know Each Other's Why

Have each person in the group share their "why" for doing the work they do. Look for similarities among the responses to this prompt. Discuss how each person's context and intention influence how they engage with their work and show up for this collaborative learning opportunity.

Activity 3: Engage With School, District, and/or State Data

To understand the relevance of homelessness to your work, engage with data from the school, district, and/or state. What are the rates of low-income students? How many students qualify for free or reduced-price lunch? How many students are identified as homeless as defined by the McKinney-Vento Act? Have these numbers changed over the past 10 years? How do these data frame how you engage with these categories?

Part I

(RE)FRAMING THE ISSUE

CHAPTER 2

The Roles and Experiences of Educators

This book focuses on exploring how to improve access to and success in PK–12 education for students experiencing homelessness and housing insecurity. Teachers, counselors, administrators, and other educators play key roles in supporting students and families, which is needed to improve both educational access and success. Schools, districts, and state coordinators should provide support to the individuals who work closely with these students and families to reduce burnout. This chapter provides a way to start conversations about what may be needed for educators to do this work; however, the exact need will be influenced by the local context.

DEFINING WHO IS AN EDUCATOR

We intentionally cast a wide net when using the term *educator*. Teachers, social workers, psychologists, counselors, office staff, lunchroom and recess staff, homeless liaisons, state coordinators, educational advocates, community partners, and administrators at the site, district, and state levels all play an important part in creating educational spaces that encourage success for all students. Each of these roles (and others that we have not listed) directly or indirectly influences how students experience their educational journeys. Educators, in our usage, are any individuals who create the context for students to learn and thrive.

We do not have the space to fully articulate all the education roles or how they positively influence students' academic experiences. As an overview, we offer the following observations:

- *Teachers* generally have the most contact with students. These educators create learning spaces and interpret curriculum to meet the needs of their students. In addition to focusing on academic content, teachers build relationships with students and families. These educators may observe or hear when a challenge exists.

- *School site staff* interact with students in many ways. Front office staff assist with registering students, answer phone calls from parents/guardians, and interact with students and parents/guardians when they stop by the office. These staff often monitor student attendance and other aspects of the student record.
- Physical education, art, music, theater, library, coaches, club supervisors, and other *specialty educators* interact with students related to these classes and activities. They may recognize a challenge that is less evident in other classes: A student may not have the appropriate apparel for the gym. An art or theater class may lead to students sharing aspects of their personal experiences.
- *Staff* who provide support with the cafeteria, recess, tutoring, transportation, and similar aspects of the school environment engage with students in informal settings. These educators may observe or hear about challenges that undermine the students' ability to fully engage in school.
- *Administrators* on site, at the district, or in county or state offices influence the experiences of the teachers, staff, students, and families. These educators have the potential to see broader trends that could be addressed. In addition, students may move between schools, and these leaders can facilitate the transition process. They provide guidance, support, and resources to achieve the site and district mission.
- *Community partners* play several roles related to supporting students and families. These educators and agencies often have resources that differ from the school's or district's. They may have a different type of relationship with the students and their families that enables them to observe their experiences in a different way.

Schools and districts are situated within a specific context. As aforementioned, our goal is not to name all the educators that exist or create a comprehensive list of all the roles they play in supporting students. Rather, we take an expansive view of who has the potential to positively influence students' educational journeys. Throughout this book, we encourage educators to think broadly about how to leverage the ideas and collaboratively work with their colleagues to improve educational outcomes. All educators in all roles have an important role to play.

IMPACT *OF* EDUCATORS

Educators generally choose this profession because they want to assist students in learning, growing, and preparing for life. Educators play a key role in supporting students' journey toward educational success. For students experiencing homelessness and housing insecurity, educators can be a vital lifeline and source of inspiration. Throughout this book, we emphasize the importance of educators. In our work, we consistently observe the positive impact that educators have had on students and their families.

As discussed further in Chapter 4, educators are most effective when they collaborate with their colleagues. The challenges that students experiencing homelessness face require multiple forms of integrated support. When educators work in collaboration, they have the potential to provide wraparound support for the students. And they can help reduce the stress that individual educators may experience by leveraging the expertise, resources, and creativity that exist across the school site, district, and state.

IMPACT *ON* EDUCATORS

The issues related to school mobility, attendance, behavior, and academic engagement create stress for educators. When students move between different schools, the educators spend time transitioning them in and out of the classroom and school. Students experiencing homelessness may move between schools during the academic year, sometimes several times a year. Each time a student enters a classroom in the middle of the school year, the teacher needs to take time assessing where the student is academically and then transitioning that student into the classroom activities. If the academic records are unavailable, this process may take longer. Given the external pressures from the district, state, and federal government, teachers may feel the need to keep the class moving and can have difficulty finding time to do a thorough assessment of each student who enters the classroom.

The process becomes more challenging as the number of students experiencing mobility increases. Having one or two students enter or leave a classroom over the course of a year may not take a significant amount of time, but some schools experience mobility rates that exceed 10% of the student population. Teachers in these classrooms have a constant flow of students in and out of the classrooms. We worked with district leaders who accept that their student population is mobile and try to proactively support schools in negotiating the challenges of serving these young people.

Caring educators can experience an emotional toll as well. Students who are homeless and highly mobile bring their lived experiences to the classroom. They may seek out teachers, counselors, and other educators when their lives are in crises. Hearing these stories can be overwhelming. Educators may have had stable home environments during their childhoods; it may be difficult for them to relate to students who endure residential instability and have experienced significant trauma. Other educators may have had similar experiences of mobility and/or trauma during their childhood. A complex array of responses may emerge for educators, including:

- They may be emotionally unable to deal with the stories students bring with them.
- They may feel the need to overcompensate for the lack of stability by lowering expectations.
- They may feel personally responsible for fixing the problem and dedicate significant extra time or resources to the students and families.
- They may be frustrated by the disruption to the class or school and feel as though a few students make it difficult to provide adequate education to the rest of the class.
- They may become numb and emotionally disconnected from the students and/or families to reduce the personal impact.

Regardless of the response, we acknowledge that student mobility can be personally challenging for teachers. In addition, differing ideas of how educators "should" respond can create tension among educators. We encourage an open dialogue to enable educators to share experiences and resources.

EDUCATORS WHO EXPERIENCE HOMELESSNESS AND HOUSING INSECURITY

Teachers, staff, and administrators are not immune from residential instability. Economic issues at the national level (e.g., the Great Recession), local level (e.g., housing shortages or natural disaster), or individual level (e.g., divorce, bankruptcy, health issue, domestic violence) can negatively impact educators. We spoke with educators who experienced residential instability while trying to maintain employment. These individuals may benefit from learning about resources available in the community.

Some educators may have experienced residential instability during their childhood and have a direct connection with and special empathy for students who are going through a similar experience. Creating safe spaces during professional development for educators to share their previous experiences may help others understand the challenges that students may be unable to articulate. These conversations allow individuals without personal experiences with poverty or homelessness to ask questions.

Educators with personal connections to poverty may feel the need to go well beyond their contractual obligations to support students experiencing homelessness. While we appreciate the commitment of these teachers, they need to be keenly aware of potential burnout. We encourage leadership to look for opportunities to support these educators' efforts while also limiting the likelihood that they become overwhelmed and leave the profession. The goal should be to extend the careers of educators. Without equipped and supported educators, students will not succeed.

PROFESSIONAL DEVELOPMENT AND COLLABORATION

We recognize that most teacher and administrative preparation programs do not include training related to homelessness or trauma-informed care. While teachers, staff, and administrators are responsible for supporting all students, the reality is that they are not necessarily trained for this work during their preparation and credential programs. We encourage colleges of education and administrative preparation programs to integrate training related to homelessness, housing insecurity, and trauma-informed approaches into their curricula in order to adequately support educators in doing this work. Meanwhile, schools and districts are responsible for giving educators the tools and philosophical orientation for supporting students—especially for those who did not get this guidance in their professional preparation programs.

One key step districts can take is to provide professional development for teachers and other staff to help them more fully understand the students' living arrangements. Doing so does not necessarily remove all the challenges of doing this work, but can provide a space for educators to brainstorm solutions within the local context. They can work with educators in other roles to create systems that enable students to enter the classroom with greater ease and more quickly identify how to obtain educational records.

EDUCATORS USING THEIR PERSONAL MONEY AND TIME TO SUPPORT STUDENTS

School teachers, staff, and leadership who become aware of the economic and residential challenges of their students often feel compelled to find ways to meet the needs they encounter each day as they interact with students. We observed several schools that organize coat and food drives to distribute to students and families who need assistance. Money might be collected to purchase gifts for students during the winter holiday season. For example, one teacher in an upper-middle-class community shared how the teachers all got together to purchase food and gifts for a student and his family who lived in a camper near the school. It is difficult to see extreme poverty and not respond. These efforts are admirable and demonstrate the ethic of care that led many educators to the profession.

We affirm the efforts of educators to meet the needs of their students and encourage them to continue doing so as they see fit. We engaged in similar efforts while working on school sites and continue to do so. By no means are we discouraging schools from serving the students and communities in these ways. However, this should not be the primary approach to supporting these young people and their families. We previously wrote about the challenges of relying *solely* on the charity of individuals in schools to support youth experiencing homelessness; we saw that doing so avoids looking at the issues that led to these tenuous and dangerous living situations (Aviles de Bradley, 2015). Educational and community leaders should collaboratively review policies and policy implementation to identify ways to provide more consistent forms of support to youth and families. A coordinated effort would enable discussions to occur that could lead to systemic changes (see Chapters 4 and 9).

In addition to encouraging efforts that could lead to broader change, we want to acknowledge the financial costs associated with relying on teachers and school staff to financially support coat closets, food drives, and holiday gifts. These efforts take a significant amount of their time to recruit individuals to donate as well as organizing and distributing the items. Some teachers and staff give a portion of their salaries to meet the needs of their students. This impacts the educators and their families, which can lead to burnout. Many educators enjoy participating in activities to support students and families. And they clearly have a positive impact on the students and help build bridges between the school and family. Ideally, these efforts are supplemental to a larger effort organized by the district or a community partner and are created in ways that do not negatively impact educators.

CHAPTER CONCLUSION

Educators play an essential role in supporting students—especially those navigating homelessness and housing instability. School often becomes a stable aspect of these young people's lives. Schools and districts need to continue exploring ways to support educators to reduce burnout. As we mention throughout this book, collaborative approaches that leverage the strengths, resources, and experiences of educators in multiple roles have the potential to reduce workload and increase effectiveness.

Guiding Questions for Individual and/or Group Reflection

1. How has your students' residential experiences and mobility impacted your work? How do you think it influences your colleagues in different roles?
2. Reflect on your current home as well as where you lived growing up. How do those experiences frame how you understand your students' experiences? What assumptions do you hold about their parents or guardians?

3. How are educators in multiple roles viewed in your school or district? Are there opportunities to increase collaboration across roles?
4. Are you feeling burnout? If so, what could colleagues do to assist? What could you do to assist your colleagues who feel burnout?

Professional Learning Community Activities

Activity 1: Understanding the Work of Colleagues

Each person gets an opportunity to (re)introduce themselves to their colleagues. Some colleagues may have worked together for several years without fully comprehending what the others do. Consider including the following:

- Provide an overview of what your work entails.
- Name challenges that exist in your role related to supporting students and families experiencing homelessness.
- Share resources or strategies that you have found effective.
- Reflect on how your personal and professional experiences frame how you approach working with students and families experiencing homelessness.

Allow colleagues to ask questions, particularly related to the first three prompts. (Asking probing questions about your colleague's personal residential experiences may not be appropriate—consider the norms that you created the first week to guide how to proceed.)

The group should keep a running list of the challenges, resources, and strategies that are identified. This information could be useful for future PLC discussions. Depending upon the challenges identified, the group should explore how to resolve those issues and/or who could be contacted to brainstorm solutions. The group may want to catalogue the resources and strategies, which could be placed in a location accessible to all educators, including those who join your school or district in the future.

Activity 2: Explore Assumptions About People Experiencing Homelessness

Give group members a few minutes to reflect the assumptions they hold related to students and families experiencing homelessness:

- What comes to mind when you hear the term *homeless*?
- Do your perceptions shift when you think about *students* experiencing homelessness?
- What experiences have you had that inform how you think about homelessness? Have you had personal experiences with housing

insecurity? How have you seen homelessness in your community or in the media?

After individually reflecting, consider how your individual and collective assumptions inform your work:

- How does your understanding or perception of homelessness influence your engagement with students and families in these situations?
- What are some strengths or assets that students and families experiencing homelessness possess? How could educators leverage the students' and family members' strengths in their practice?

CHAPTER 3

Defining Diverse Homeless Experiences

As most educational leaders can attest, poverty looks different depending upon the geographic and social context. For example, urban and rural poverty involve distinct challenges. The amount of money that qualifies a person as "low-income" or "in poverty" depends upon the cost of living in a particular community. A person making $50,000 in a small town in Nebraska will have a different lifestyle than a person making the same amount in Chicago or Miami. Similarly, homelessness can manifest itself in different ways in different communities and contexts. How students experience homelessness influences their educational experiences.

In this chapter, we provide definitions and illustrations of the diverse ways that young people and their families experience residential instability and mobility. While it would be impossible to articulate every possible way that homelessness presents itself, our goal is to help educators to think about how these issues may look locally. This discussion is intended to broaden notions of homelessness, not create an exhaustive list.

In the sections that follow, we discuss different forms of homelessness that schools and districts encounter (National Center for Homeless Education, 2024; Tierney et al., 2008). As will become obvious, the categories are not discrete and tend to be fluid. The reality is that the experiences of youth and families frequently overlap the categories or are situated somewhere in between. Students often go through more than one episode of residential instability and experience multiple forms of homelessness. Understanding the various ways that homelessness exists for students and their families is an important foundation to begin considering how to create support in the local context.

DIFFERENT TYPES OF HOMELESSNESS AMONG STUDENTS

McKinney-Vento specifically outlines different residential contexts that qualify a student to receive educational support (see Chapter 5). While these students share an overarching experience of residential instability, how this occurs differs depending on the specific context. In the subsections that follow, we explain and illustrate how unstable residential arrangements frame the education experiences of youth.

Categories of Residential Status

Shelters: Youth residing in emergency, short-term, or long-term shelter. This includes young people who are with or without their family. These shelters can be a great distance from the home school.

Disconnected: Youth under the age of 18 living with their family or on their own in a car, abandoned building, campsite, or place not suitable for nighttime residence. These families do not receive social service resources and school attendance is sporadic.

Public Spaces: Youth who seek refuge in high-risk, nontraditional locations, such as under bridges, in bus or train stations, on park benches, and in abandoned buildings or other public spaces. They are generally disconnected from services for homeless youth and disengaged from the educational system.

Hotels/motels: Families living in a hotel or motel due to economic hardship. "Welfare hotels" involve subpar living conditions, including no access to a kitchen and public bathrooms shared by multiple tenants. Each room may have in excess of five people sharing a space designed for one person.

Couch surfing: Youth who ask friends, family, or acquaintances to allow them to sleep at their house—typically on the floor or a couch. Securing a place to sleep each night takes a great deal of time and energy away from educational engagement.

Doubled-up: Families sharing space with another family due to economic hardship. The crowded environment affords only a semi-stable situation; if there is a dispute or one family experiences a financial crisis, all residents potentially end up without a home. These residences may have two families or more sharing a space typically designed for one family.

Shelters

Shelters for individuals who lack residential stability exist in many communities. These organizations serve individuals experiencing crises and tend to be a last resort for families. Most urban areas have a shortage of available bed space as compared to the need. Often cities have less than half the number of shelter beds required to serve the local need. These shelters are funded using social welfare or private funding. Only 40% of families living in a shelter find permanent housing within a year (National Alliance to End Homelessness, 2020).

Who can access these beds and how long a person can stay varies depending upon the structure and focus of the specific shelter. The services available to youth within these different spaces depend in large part on the structural design and focus. Although shelters can be designed in different ways, we discuss four common types: emergency, family, youth, and domestic violence shelters.

Emergency shelters often exist in urban areas, particularly near the city center. These facilities provide a space for individuals without housing for a single night at a time. While individuals can seek refuge in these spaces for more than one night, the bed is not guaranteed from one day to the next. Often, the number of beds available meets only a fraction of the need within a given community. Those wishing to receive a shower, meal, and bed may need to line up several hours before the doors open to be sure they will have shelter for that night. The sleeping arrangements generally involve a large open space with each person assigned a cot or a bed. Residents need to leave after breakfast each morning and take all their belongings with them. Getting into the shelter each night requires dedicating significant time each afternoon waiting for the facility to open, and safeguarding belongings can be difficult (and embarrassing) to manage while at work or school during the day. This can create obvious challenges for an individual trying to secure employment or for a student attempting to attend school. In addition, young people have a difficult time participating in afterschool events if they need to be at the shelter to secure a space to sleep that night.

These shelters tend to be divided, with males over a certain age (the division is usually somewhere between the ages of 13 and 18) in one space or building, and women and children in a separate space or building. Many directors of these facilities argue that this is done to protect the residents from physical or sexual assault. They fear having adult males sleeping and showering in close proximity with females and children. The unintended consequences include separating families, which discourages some people from seeking refuge in the shelter. For example, a single father may not feel comfortable having his children in a different building and, as a result, may not take advantage of the shelter or its resources. Similarly, a mother may be nervous about her teenage son being out of her supervision. These policies put the onus of parenting on mothers, which can place additional pressure on a romantic relationship that is already experiencing stresses associated with residential instability.

A young person who is unaccompanied may choose to avoid these shelters. Being in a large facility with individuals navigating mental illness and addictions can be scary for an unaccompanied teenager. Shelters can also be difficult for gender-nonconforming individuals. Transgender and queer individuals may feel uncomfortable fitting within the imposed gender binary and may experience discrimination or violence in these open living spaces.

While emergency shelters meet immediate needs for individuals who need shelter, they are not intended to be a nurturing space for long-term living. Sadly, many of the residents seek refuge night after night in these shelters because there tend to be even fewer spaces in long-term shelters and transitional housing programs. The constant uncertainty inherent in having to reapply daily for nightly housing can affect young people psychologically, and being obliged to move from one place to another can make it hard for a student merely to get to a school on a regular basis.

Family shelters are designed to support family units. These facilities may be short-term (e.g., 30 to 60 days) or long-term (e.g., 6 to 24 months). The short-term shelters tend to focus on helping the family find a more stable residence with some modest other support. The long-term programs function more like wraparound support that provide the family with multiple resources, including helping the parents or guardians acquire skills needed to access gainful employment. Instead of sleeping in a large open space, the families often have an individual room or a space similar to an apartment. Residents in family shelters typically work with a case manager who assists with identifying resources that could help them become residentially stable. These wraparound programs attempt to address all the issues influencing the family's financial and residential insecurity. The goal is to create a plan that will enable parents to secure financial stability while also supporting their children in remaining engaged with school.

How *family* is defined varies depending upon the shelter's mission and funding. The shelter may have a narrow definition of family as a mother, father, or partnership with their biological children. Or a broader definitional approach may be taken that includes grandparents, aunts/uncles, and other family formations that may not be biological. Most often, these shelters involve supporting individuals caring for children. The adults are required to work, attend school, and/or engage in a training program to remain at the facility. These programs typically assist in transitioning to low-income housing with the goal of achieving future stability. Often, these shelters also have space for the students to complete homework and may have a tutoring program.

Youth shelters focus on providing support for young people who are not living with a parent or guardian. Some shelters focus on young people under the age of 18; these facilities generally collaborate with social services and foster care systems. Most often, the youth are in middle or high school—rarely are elementary-aged children placed in youth shelters. Although the youth may initially seek refuge at the facility without being in the foster care system, the staff is legally obligated to contact social services to report the unaccompanied minor. For young people fleeing the foster care system, this legal requirement may be an obstacle. Other shelters support young people who are transitioning to adulthood—the age range varies, but usually within the range of 18 to 24 years of age. These programs generally focus on young people who do not have the support of a guardian. Generally speaking, the young person needs to be in school or job training or working while at the facility. The agency assists with transitioning to permanent housing. Youth programs may have a specialized focus, such as working with former foster youth. The exact age range and focus of support vary depending upon the state and local context.

Youth shelters require young people to move out once they reach a certain age. One important note: Most youth shelters do not serve individuals both under and over 18. As a result, turning 18 often results in loss of shelter. In the best-case scenario, the young person transitions from one youth shelter to another with a higher age limit. Unfortunately, that is not always easy or possible.

Domestic violence shelters typically support women fleeing abusive relationships. Some shelters serve men, but this is rare. Women may bring children with them to the shelter. Domestic violence shelters often have an office space that is publicly advertised, but the actual shelter is in a discreet location to protect the residents from their abusers. The length of stay varies. The overarching goal is to protect the residents until they can be transitioned to a permanent and safe living arrangement. These programs partner with community organizations or advocates that help residents take legal steps to protect themselves and their children from future violence.

The young people may continue at the same school if it is determined to be safe and in their best interest to go to a place that is known to the abuser. Frequently, students miss school while the case manager works to stabilize the family and ensure that everyone is safe. Most often, the young person becomes disconnected from the previous school and relationships. If the abuser is incarcerated or otherwise prevented from harming the child, the child may return to the previous school. These children and their families experience a significant amount of uncertainty, disconnection, and fear as they transition out of the abusive situation.

The above summaries provide a sense of the diversity of shelters available for youth and families. In addition to providing a bed, the facility may or may not have other services available. Some have study rooms for students to do homework and others have volunteer tutors come by a few times a week. However, shelters tend to focus on meeting the immediate needs of a place to sleep for the night and, secondarily, transitioning the residents to more permanent living arrangements. Some shelters assist with transportation to school by providing a van, but the kids often experience shame if their peers see them getting out of a van with the shelter's name on the side. Most often, the families are responsible for figuring out how to get the children to school. In some cases, the shelters can be a great distance from the student's home school.

Disconnected and Public Spaces

Youth who are disconnected live outside of typical residential contexts. These youth may or may not have familial connections. These individuals tend to live at the fringes of communities in spaces that are not visible, such as cars, abandoned buildings, campsites, or other places that are not adequate. The exposed nature of these living arrangements leaves young people vulnerable to violence and other forms of abuse. These youth typically do not receive significant support from social service agencies that may assist with food or permanent housing. School attendance tends to be sporadic at best.

A few groups of unaccompanied students are overrepresented among disconnected youth, for example, LGBTQ+ youth forced to leave their family homes or individuals fleeing domestic violence situations. Youth who have run away from foster care placements might also end up disconnected, since they are wary of connecting with social service or educational institutions that may return them to foster care placement. These youth may seek refuge in high-risk, nontraditional locations, such as under bridges, in bus or train stations, on park benches, or in abandoned buildings or other public spaces.

Young people in these situations are generally disconnected from social services and disengage from the educational system. They also may have a difficult time attending to hygiene, which may discourage them from attending school (see Ruth's story of living in a storage room). In addition, they experience high rates of abuse while negotiating residential instability. These young people frequently develop networks among other youth and adults living on the street.

Living in a Storage Room

Ruth, a 16-year-old Latina, enjoys the social aspects of high school. She eagerly talks about her friends and shares how she really likes a young man who plays on the football team. She plans to finish high school and then become a cosmetologist. Her eyes turn away and her voice softens as she discusses how she lives with her mother, brother, and grandmother in a storage room behind a church.

Basic needs take priority over school. With the assistance of a church leader, they sneak into the room by 6:00 p.m., where they stay until early in the morning; they have to be secretive and leave before others are around in order to avoid being reported to the police for living in a nonresidential location. They fill two buckets with water each afternoon: one for drinking and cleaning, the other for a toilet. Bathing becomes difficult; occasionally, the gym teacher lets Ruth use the school shower. Given the social pressures and shame Ruth experiences, she attends school only on the days that she can shower. "You might think it's dumb, but I just like to be clean." She pauses. "Most days I don't even shower."

Ruth's dream is to have "a home where I could take a shower, you know, brush my teeth in a real sink. Actually flush the toilet, you know. I would want at least an apartment, I'm not asking for a big mansion, at least a small apartment."

Hotels, Motels, and Single Room Occupancies

Families may seek refuge in hotels or motels because of economic hardship. These businesses rent rooms by the week or month at low rates. These rooms generally serve as long-term housing. Unlike the hotels that middle-class individuals visit during vacations or business trips, these so-called "welfare hotels" involve subpar living conditions. The families rarely have access to a kitchen or living spaces beyond the bedroom where the family resides, and the rooms may not have a small refrigerator to store food. Families who can afford it often purchase a hot plate to cook meals.

Some spaces are structured as single room occupancies (SROs) where the living space (e.g., 10' by 12' room with bunk beds) has one bathroom for all the residents on a floor to share. These may be former hotels that were converted for long-term, low-income tenants. SROs can be dangerous spaces because of increased exposure to substance use and violence. These buildings tend to be run by landlords who do not adequately take care of facilities, and the history of SROs shows a significant amount of tenant abuse by the property owners.

Families living in hotels, motels, or SROs tend to be disconnected from social services—in part because the owner may make it difficult for outsiders to enter the building where subpar living conditions could be exposed and reported. The residents can be evicted without notice for any reason. The buildings are often overcrowded (see Franklin's experience living in a hotel). For example, a family of four or more people may live in a single room. The locations rarely have outdoor spaces for children to play, which can create additional stress on the family, as everyone is compressed into a small space. In addition, finding a space to complete homework can be nearly impossible.

Living in a Hotel

I recently lived in Skid Row where I saw a lot of things, both good and bad. One of the good things is I had a lot of friends. One of the bad things is I saw a lot of people throw their lives away by smoking crack, prostitution, and murder. Most of that stuff takes place in the hotels where families live.

My family stayed in a hotel; about 300 people lived in there with us. The rooms were small, about the same size of a walk-in closet, but my family and I had two rooms. Six people lived in the two rooms; we had two bunk beds. Two of my sisters slept on the bottom of one bunk. My other sister slept right above them on the top bunk. My mom and my little brother slept on the bottom of the second bunk, and I slept right above them. We had a hot plate so we could cook and we had a mini refrigerator to keep our food good. The small bathrooms were in the hallway, and we had to share them with 300 people; people got sick a lot.

There were a lot of kids and all of them were my friends. Living down there got me stronger because it numbed me up, but now I'm immune to most stuff that is harder for other people. After seeing my friend's mom get killed on the side of the hotel I made a documentary.

—Franklin, 16 years old

Couch Surfers

Youth who couch surf are typically disconnected from their parents or a guardian. These young people ask friends, family, and acquaintances to allow them to sleep at their home for a night or maybe a couple of nights. Securing a place to sleep each night takes a great deal of time and energy away from educational engagement. The consistent requests for support may create pressure on the students' relationships either because of the shame associated with continuously telling friends about not having a place to stay or because the friends get tired of being asked and start avoiding the student. Instead of seeing friendships as a means of social support, these students also use them for residential refuge.

These youth may attend school, in part, to remain connected to a social network that may assist with locating a place to sleep each night. The location of their housing could be a great distance from school and figuring out transportation can be challenging, since the location of their residence changes so often. Youth who are couch surfing are rarely connected with social service agencies or an adult who may be providing guidance. As a result, their ability to access resources or permanent housing is severely limited. When their social network gets exhausted, these young people frequently end up living on the street or seeking refuge at a homeless shelter.

Couch Surfing

A young woman we worked with explained how she resorted to offering to work for her friends' parents in return for shelter. She ended up finding a friend's mother who agreed to let her sleep on the couch in exchange for cleaning the house. While this living arrangement was modestly more stable than when she was moving from place to place each night, she also knew that at any moment her housing could end. For example, she had to exit when the family had people visiting town. After a couple of months, the family got tired of having her taking up the space in the living room and she was back to searching for a place to stay.

Doubled-Up

The first step for many families who lose residential stability often involves seeking refuge in the home of a friend or family member. Before most individuals reach a homeless shelter, they have spent extended periods of time living in the homes of other individuals. When their social networks become exhausted, the individuals tend to move into their vehicles or seek the assistance of shelters. Nearly 76% of the students categorized as homeless by schools and districts live in doubled-up residences (National Center for Homeless Education, 2024). This is the largest, and often most misunderstood, subgroup of students experiencing homelessness (Hallett, 2012a, 2012b). A doubled-up residence is when two or more households live within a space designed for one housed as a result of economic crises.

Some doubled-up residences involve an individual or family staying with a friend who has stable housing. Other doubled-up residences involve multiple households that lack the ability to live independently residing in the same apartment or house (see Rosie's story). These arrangements can provide more space and security than other forms of homelessness, but the stability is precarious. If one of the households experience financial stress, all the households likely lose housing because the ability to pay rent and utilities is contingent on all households contributing.

These residences may have more than three families sharing a space designed for one family. Families in doubled-up residences share space with another family due to economic hardship, not solely for cultural preferences. The possibility exists that a family could choose to live with extended family; however, the residence qualifies as doubled-up when economic limitations force multiple households to live in a dwelling designed for only one residence. The crowded environment only affords a semi-stable situation (see Appendix A for further illustration of doubled-up residences).

Rosie Lives Doubled-Up

In elementary school, Rosie lived with her parents and two siblings in a middle-class neighborhood. As she was entering middle school, her father lost his job and her parents got a divorce. Her mother moved with her children into a family member's home for a few months and sought support from social services. She eventually moved into a studio apartment, which was all she could afford, with the three kids.

A few years later, a woman with two young children moved into a studio apartment down the hall. The families became friends and realized they could pool their resources. They found a small three-bedroom apartment that enabled both mothers to have their own room and the five children shared the third bedroom. While clearly not adequate space, the doubled-up residence provided more space than the two studio apartments. The families now had a living room, dining space and kitchen. In addition, Rosie's mom helped to coordinate getting all the children to and from school while the other mother worked two jobs to help provide for the two families.

When we met Rosie, she was a junior in high school and the oldest of the children in the home. She loved her family and appreciated how their new residence enabled her to have more space to spend with them. However, she had a hard time sleeping in a 10x10 room that had two bunk beds and a pull-out mattress for her brother. The five children each had a plastic bin with their clothes and other items stacked in the corner. Each morning, they would need to shuffle the bins as they got ready for school. Finding a place to do homework was challenging, since there was always someone in the bedroom and the small dining room table sat only two people. In the second semester of her senior year, the other family had saved enough money to move into another location. Her mother was uncertain what to do next. They considered moving into a family shelter located on the other side of the city, which would make it difficult for Rosie to continue at the same school.

HOMELESSNESS IS NOT ALL THE SAME

Despite the common experience of disruption to housing stability experienced by children and youth identified as homeless, all experiences of homelessness are not the same. Furthermore, schools and districts are not equally prepared to work in partnerships with children and families who are or have been homeless. As Pavlakis (2015) found, the setting matters. Her study examined the perceptions of school personnel and parents experiencing homelessness in urban areas. She differentiated her results based on the type of setting the families lived in—traditional homeless shelter, "housing-first" community-supplied residential spaces, or doubled-up families who lived with other family units in residences designed for single families. She found a disconnect between school personnel's perceptions of parents' abilities to support school efforts (such as supervising homework and attending school events) and the perceptions of the parents themselves. The school personnel tended to view the doubled-up situations as the best option, but the parents held different views:

> A school social worker explained how "the kids that are going in and out of different motels and shelters struggle . . . they struggle a little bit more," compared with "the families that are doubled up [who] seem to be a bit more stable." However, most [homeless and highly mobile] parents commented that doubling up was the "most stressful time" for themselves and their children. One parent reported that doubling up was dangerous for her young children because she could not childproof someone else's home. (p. 21)

This research builds on what Hallett (2012a, 2012b) and others have found; in effect, that the challenges of children and families experiencing homelessness are often hidden, overlooked, poorly understood, misunderstood, or ignored by schools and districts.

The responses and solutions local educational agencies formulate for these families' challenges may be poorly matched and ineffective given the local needs of the youth and families within the community. Also, the functionality of the school–family relationship for this student population varies widely based on other factors, such as the age of the child, the coexistence of special learning needs, and the presence or absence of other community support agencies. This is the reason for our call for redesign of educational programming with the needs in mind of children, youth, and families experiencing homelessness, high mobility, and residential instability (see Chapter 4).

A Middle School Principal Broadens Their Definition of Homelessness

I think it's a shift in what they [district leadership] thought of as homeless, that it wasn't just a student who says—because we have them that are staying at a hotel or they're living out of their car. It was ones that were not living in their own home. When that shift happens of how they define homelessness, that's when we started realizing, "Oh my gosh, we have a lot of kids in this situation." There's a challenge when you're living somewhere and it's not your home. We're kind of seeing that with parents. Other kids' parents would want to come pick up kids. Then they wouldn't be on the list. Then we'd have to call the parent on the list. We're pretty flexible in terms of if they're not on the list and we can get ahold of someone that is and they give permission, then we let it happen. We're not going to deny someone picking up the kid as long as we can get verification that it's okay. We're seeing a lot of that happening. How the district changed that, I'm not sure where that shift came from the district's perspective.

CHAPTER CONCLUSION

We want to acknowledge how overwhelming this social issue can feel. Given the many challenges these students face, it can seem that education may be the least of their concerns. Clearly, the federal, state, and local governments need to find additional ways to increase affordable housing and other social service supports for these children and their families. However, education plays a significant role in helping these young people gain the knowledge and skills they will need to achieve long-term stability. We need to find ways for them to continue engaging in school even while they negotiate finding a stable residence. Fortunately, there are several steps that educators can implement to support students in homeless situations.

Guiding Questions for Individual and/or Group Reflection

1. How do students and families in your classroom, school, and/or district experience homelessness? How do different residence types influence the ways these students engage with school?
2. Reflect on your individual work. Are there ways to integrate what you have learned into your work? Are there policies and practices that could be shifted?

Professional Learning Community Activities

Activity 1: Engaging With Data

Review data related to student residences for your school, district, and/or state. Most districts and states require schools to use a student residency questionnaire (SRQ) or similar tool to gather information needed to identify students who are homeless.

- Review the tool used to gather data. Are there revisions needed to the tool based upon what you learned? Does the process of distributing the SRQ to students and families need to be adjusted to ensure accurate data and access to resources?
- What categories of homelessness occur most frequently?
- Do the data reflect your experiences as an educator in the school, district, or state?
- How does this information inform your practice and the work of your colleagues?

Activity 2: Engaging With Community

Create a map of the different locations where students and families live in your local community. Consider including the following:

- Homeless and domestic violence shelters
- Hotels, motels, and single room occupancies
- Housing projects; public housing
- Buildings or areas where families live doubled-up—this may be more difficult to assess

Discuss what educators know about these different aspects of the community:

- Does the school or district have a relationship with the individuals who run shelters, hotels, motels, and public housing? If not, would it be possible to build those relationships?
- Does the school or district have relationships with the social service agencies that support families in these residences? If not, would it be possible to build those relationships?

Activity 3: Visualizing Doubled-Up Residences

For most schools, districts, and states, doubled-up residences represented over half of the youth experiencing homelessness. These residences tend to be invisible to educators. Review Appendix A, which provides two illustrations of students who live in doubled-up residences. Also, consider Rosie's vignette presented earlier in this chapter. Discuss the following:

- Do families in your classroom, school, or district live doubled-up? What do those residences look like?
- How could living doubled-up influence students' ability to complete assignments, attend schools, participate in extracurriculars, or otherwise engage with the educational process?
- How does your school and district gather reliable data to understand if students live doubled-up? What policies or practices serve as barriers to adequately identifying and serving students?
- What community resources exist to support students living doubled-up?

CHAPTER 4

Rethinking Educational Approaches

Students who are homeless, like all students, need a solid educational foundation to achieve future stability and life success. How districts, schools, and teachers structure the educational process for these students has the potential to positively influence their academic achievement. Some schools and districts begin by primarily focusing on helping students get enrolled to attend school without developing and putting in place the supports that students need in order to succeed once they complete the registration process. Consider this description of the problem provided by one of our research participants who was a high school student experiencing residential instability:

> I been through a homeless shelter and all of that stuff . . . like my life like changed . . . Last year I had honors English, good stuff, but now I don't want to come to school, my grades are going down . . . It's making me feel like I can't learn, 'cause I got a lot of stuff going on in my head. (Aviles de Bradley, 2015, p. 32)

This student's experiences with homelessness affected her mental health and ability to learn. Ensuring access to school is a first step, but additional forms of support will be needed for the student to thrive.

Residential insecurity undermines a young person's perception of safety and stability. For most students, this becomes a form of trauma that can negatively impact their educational engagement. In this chapter, we argue that holistic support for students addresses their complex needs, goals, and experiences. To support students holistically, educators must see the potential in each student and take responsibility for helping them to achieve. This involves leveraging trauma-informed practices to address the reality that housing insecurity and homelessness is a form of trauma. Based upon these foundations, we offer a new approach for educators—an ecology of promise—that can be used to create supportive experiences for students and can realign how educators engage with each other to provide support.

While we focus on how an ecology of promise approach can be useful in supporting students experiencing homelessness, we must also say that this approach has the potential to benefit *all* students. Shifting school or district policies and practices to benefit just one subgroup of students can be challenging. Educators can explore how the ecology of promise approach could be used to explore how to support other subgroups of students (e.g., youth in foster care, students with special needs, or low-income students) as well as leveraging this approach to assess overall school or district practices.

Before we proceed, we want to acknowledge that many educators feel overworked and burned out. Taking on a new approach can feel like more work without more compensation. As with any meaningful change, there will be a learning curve at the start, but our approach gives educators a new research-informed way to do things, not more tasks to complete. Our approach leverages collective and collaborative action; working together can reduce the burden on individual educators while improving outcomes. Schools or districts that adopt this approach may also find that teachers feel more supported because they are not trying to meet all the needs of the students in their classrooms by themselves. In the sections that follow, we discuss the foundations of this new approach before discussing how to create an ecology of promise.

SUPPORTING THE WHOLE STUDENT

Students experiencing homelessness arrive at a school with goals, identities, and experiences that frame how they engage with educators, peers, and classwork. Some of these students may be in gifted and talented education (GATE), special education, English language learner (ELL) programs, or other supplemental education programs. Students may have athletic, musical, theatrical, scientific, public speaking, or many other talents that they bring with them to school. Just because a student is homeless does not mean they do not have goals or that all their previous experiences and relationships have been bad. These students are more similar to their peers than they are different, and they benefit from being able to bring their full selves to school and the classroom. However, given the significant challenges that a student without residential stability may experience, these individual strengths may not be immediately evident. The overarching purpose of this discussion is to encourage educators to think holistically about students and not assume that they all have the same backgrounds and experiences.

Most students experiencing homelessness have long-term academic and career goals that involve graduating from high school and pursuing a postsecondary degree or credential. They generally want to build personal relationships and feel connected to a community of support. In the short term, they may want to make friends, join clubs, play sports, or engage in other extracurricular activities. These goals and aspirations typically evolve and develop as they navigate school and grow older.

Students also bring their whole selves with them to school. Each student has a personality and disposition that frames how they engage with and experience school. Being from a rural, suburban, or urban area—including where they previously lived and where they live now—can shape the student's perspective. The student's racial and/or ethnic identity often influences how they engage with school and, potentially, how educators and peers engage with them. Similarly, a student's sex, gender, and sexual identity often shape how they experience the social and academic aspects of a school. And a student's religious views and connection (or not) to a religious community frequently influences how they experience the educational context. There are likely other aspects of a student that also shape their experiences—our goal is not to create an exhaustive list, but to highlight the importance of creating space for the students to bring their full self to the educational context and consider how these aspects of self may influence the student's experiences of homelessness and housing insecurity. Recognizing these different aspects of the student may also allow educators to explore how to connect with current or potential support systems—for example, a church or synagogue may provide resources for young people.

In addition, students experiencing homelessness bring their previous experiences, in the educational system and elsewhere, with them. Their interactions with other teachers and schools generally shape how they engage. Some may have had overwhelmingly positive encounters with administrators, teachers, staff, and peers, while others may bring negative experiences that result in their inability to trust that school is a safe space. These students may have had relationships within the educational system disrupted by their residential mobility. Similarly, their relationships with family may be a complex mix of loving and supportive and, at times, harmful or disruptive. These students often have had multiple different housing experiences that may or may not have been positive. And, unfortunately, some students will bring with them emotional, physical, sexual, and/or psychological trauma. The unstable and potentially dangerous environments these youth negotiate may warrant additional access to counseling and support services. These students and their families often need access to mental health services and support to deal with the chronic low-grade stress of residential instability in addition to other issues that contribute to students experiencing complex trauma daily. In fact,

> homeless adolescents report significantly high rates of mental health problems, substance use, and trauma histories (e.g., Merscham, Van Leeuwen, & McGuire, 2009). Moreover, homeless adolescents are at great risk of becoming chronically homeless adults if their mental health and behavioral problems are not addressed. (Milburn et al., 2017, p. 37)

Thus, addressing mental needs is an essential part of seeing a student holistically rather than as existing in a single category.

We encourage educators to provide holistic support that considers multiple aspects of the student and their experiences. For example, a student on the verge of dropping out might have been an honors student the year prior to losing housing. The potential exists to leverage these positive academic experiences as sources of strength when developing a plan of action. Considering a student holistically also enables them to feel seen and heard, which may be an important step in rebuilding their trust of the educational system.

CONSIDERING STUDENTS AT-PROMISE

The language used to identify students frames how they perceive themselves as well as how educators think about the students and what they may be capable of accomplishing. Much of the language historically used to name students who experience academic challenges assumes a deficit within the student. For example, many schools and districts have used the term *at-risk* to identify student subgroups with historically lower outcomes. The term has been used to name risks and attempt to develop resources to meet their needs. We affirm these educators' interest in improving the educational experiences and outcomes of students. However, terms like at-risk focus almost exclusively on the assumed challenges students face without also prioritizing their strengths and potential. We join a growing group of educators and researchers who argue for strengths-oriented language.

The term *at-promise* has two benefits (see Figure 4.1)—it encourages educators to think holistically about the multiple aspects of the student and it makes clear educators' commitment to supporting students (Bettencourt et al., 2023). We should be clear: We are not arguing for another label to be added to students experiencing homelessness or other subgroups of students. Rather, our goal is to adjust the overarching framing of how students are perceived. Considering students as at-promise shifts how educators approach their work.

First, the term *at-promise* encourages educators, schools, and other institutions to see students' potential instead of focusing primarily on their risk factors. While an individual student may have a host of issues or experiences that may be challenging their ability to succeed, that does not mean they do not have promise. They possess the potential to succeed academically and personally—both now and in the future. However, they may need additional support to achieve those goals. As discussed in the previous section, educators can holistically engage with students to leverage their strengths while also addressing challenges. This connects to the second aspect of promise: Educators, schools, and other institutions *promise* or commit to provide the support that students need to achieve their full potential. Schools, districts, and community organizations should leverage their resources to guide and assist the students they serve.

Figure 4.1. Considering Students as "At-Promise"

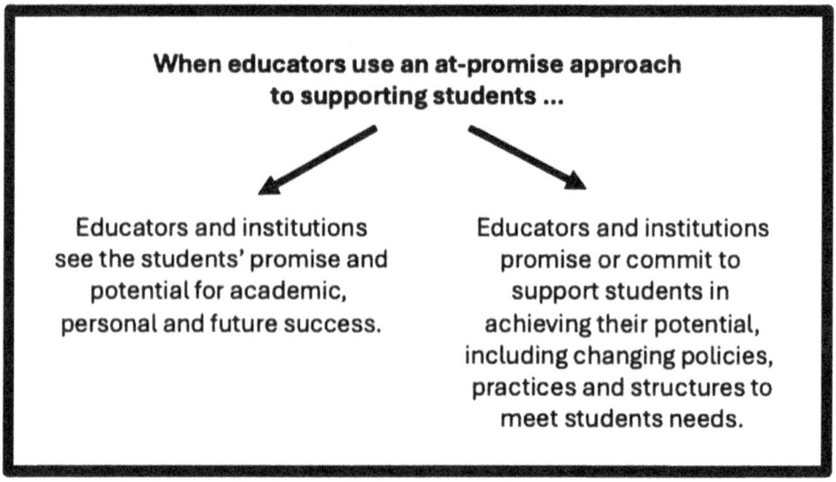

When educators use an at-promise approach to supporting students ...

Educators and institutions see the students' promise and potential for academic, personal and future success.

Educators and institutions promise or commit to support students in achieving their potential, including changing policies, practices and structures to meet students needs.

Adapted from Hallett et al., 2024.

Considering students experiencing homelessness as at-promise may involve shifts in how individuals, schools, and districts think about their students. Some narratives about students experiencing homelessness suggest that they are destined to fail and have too many barriers to be successful, and that individual students who do succeed are exceptions who triumph over expectations. An at-promise mindset begins with the assumption that these students can be successful and that the adults in their lives can assist them in reaching their full potential.

USING TRAUMA-INFORMED PRACTICES

As aforementioned, homelessness and housing insecurity are traumatic experiences for youth. Students in these situations may endure multiple forms of trauma depending upon their specific experiences. Educators are more effective if they understand the complex cognitive, psychological, and physical effects that both acute and chronic trauma have on children and youth. As Hopper and colleagues (2010) explained:

> Few programs serving homeless individuals and families directly address the specialized needs of trauma survivors. Homeless services have a long history of serving trauma survivors, without being aware of or addressing the impact of traumatic stress. Overwhelmed by the daily needs of their clients, providers in these settings often have few resources to address issues of long-term recovery. (p. 81)

Some educators have long known that the way they work with students who live in traumatic circumstances makes a dramatic difference for these students' classroom experiences in the short term and for their future in the long term.

In this section, we provide an overview of trauma-informed practices. We highlight practices associated with schools and districts that employ a trauma-informed approach. Several resources exist related to trauma-informed approaches to education—we mention a few that could be incorporated into professional development activities. While we focus on how trauma-informed practice can be effective with students experiencing homelessness, it should be noted that these techniques have been successful when used with all subgroups of students.

What Is Trauma-Informed Practice?

The impact of homelessness or frequent dislocation is nothing less than traumatic. People experiencing trauma often focus on survival. Typical responses include fight, flight, or freeze. A student experiencing trauma may bring these defense mechanisms with them to school, which can undermine their ability to fully engage with educators and peers. These coping strategies may be counterproductive in the classroom and playground. A student experiencing trauma may appear to be a "troublemaker" or "loner"—which becomes an identity that frames their interactions with teachers, staff, administrators, and peers.

Trauma-informed practice begins by naming and acknowledging that trauma exists and frames how individuals engage with systems. Trauma-informed care typically leverages several principles to create a strategy for addressing challenges that students may experience (see Table 4.1). These characteristics of trauma-informed practices may look different in each educational setting.

Characteristics of Schools and Districts That Integrate Trauma-Informed Practices

Schools and districts that leverage trauma-informed practices examine virtually every aspect of their educational programs and align them with the principles above. Ingram and colleagues (2016) suggest that it is important to "provide training to staff to ensure that classrooms and schools are trauma sensitive, so that students feel more supported and comfortable to come forward and self-identify" (p. 41). This process could happen simultaneously with the policy and practice reviews mandated by McKinney-Vento and ESSA.

Some traditional school operations may unintentionally retraumatize already traumatized individuals through lack of understanding, insufficient empathy, poor training, inattention, poor communication, deficit attitudes,

Table 4.1. Principles and Strategies Associated With Trauma-Informed Care

Principle	Strategy
Understand trauma and its impact	Provide educators with ongoing information and training on trauma and its effects
Promote safety	All programming and procedures are designed to support the school as a safe and caring space
Ensure holistic support	Develop competence in understanding how trauma may be experienced differently for students depending on their background and identities
Support student choice and autonomy	Include students and families in decision-making, implementation, and evaluation of programs as appropriate
Share power and governance	Shared power and control over participation with schools is the goal rather than the typical "power over" situation families experiencing homelessness find themselves in
Integrate care	Youth experiencing homelessness typically have multiple needs, and collaboratively integrating care must be a priority
Believe that relationships are central to healing	This belief must guide the development and review of policies, practices, and procedures designed to support students and families
Understand that recovery is possible	People's housing situations and mental health states can and do improve, and schools can play vital roles in making recovery possible

Adapted from Steele & Malchiodi, 2012, pp. 16–17.

and so forth. Organizational values drive the factors that produce these aspects of school practice. The values associated with trauma-informed practice include safety, trustworthiness, choice, collaboration, and empowerment (Steele & Malchiodi, 2012). The shift can be illustrated by the difference between the questions "What's wrong with you?" versus "What has happened to you?" (Health Care for the Homeless Clinicians' Network, 2010).

Moving a school or district toward meeting students' and families' needs in a safe, supportive environment that holds high expectations for all learners and believes in hope and possibility may be a significant undertaking. It requires excellent leadership and long-term commitment to professional learning, assessment, evaluation, and accountability. As Steele and Malchiodi (2012) noted: "Too often programs 'adapt the language' but fail to understand the role that process plays in helping staff with major paradigm shifts" (p. 123).

Professional Development Resources Related to Trauma-Informed Practices

The National Center for Homeless Education has curated several free resources for educators (https://nche.ed.gov/trauma/). We highlight a few; however, we encourage educators to browse the site for additional resources that may be useful.

- *A Long Journey Home: A Guide for Creating Trauma-Informed Services for Mothers and Children Experiencing Homelessness*—provides practical ideas and practices related to creating a trauma-informed environment.
- *Child Trauma Toolkit for Educators*—the toolkit (in English and Spanish) includes a variety of resources geared toward multiple audiences, including parents and guardians, related to working with youth who have experienced trauma.
- *Implementing Trauma-Informed Practices in Rural Schools*—considers the specific aspects of developing and implementing trauma-informed approaches within rural contexts.
- *Trauma-Informed Organizational Capacity Scale*—tool developed to assess the capacity and effectiveness of programs proving trauma-informed care for students experiencing homelessness.
- *Understanding Trauma and Its Impact*—training resources for schools and districts, including interactive e-resources, slide decks, and activities.

CREATING AN ECOLOGY OF PROMISE—A NEW APPROACH

In the previous sections, we argue for holistically considering the students' experiences and backgrounds; leveraging an at-promise mindset; and utilizing trauma-informed approaches. Using these concepts as a foundation, we present a new approach to supporting students: creating an *ecology of promise*. This is a research-informed approach that draws from previous work to argue for an institutional culture shift in how schools engage with students (Hallett et al., 2023; Kezar et al., 2024; Kitchen et al., 2021).

The idea of being *student-centered* has become a common refrain in education. However, few frameworks exist to provide guidance for educators in implementing student-centered practices. An ecology of promise (see Figure 4.2) involves leveraging the concepts presented in this chapter to be student-centered. This involves rebalancing policies, practices, and structures to prioritize the needs and goals of students who experience homelessness. The process involves moving away from individual educator efforts and toward building an ecology of support that includes educators in the

Figure 4.2. Ecology of Promise Norms

Ecology of Promise Norms

Norms for How Educators Engage with Students:	Norms for How Educators Engage with Each Other:
• Proactive	• Collaborative
• Holistic	• Reflective
• Developmental	
• Strengths-oriented	

school, district, and community working collaboratively. Educators will need to identify and evaluate institutional norms that frame how educators and schools engage with students as well as the way that they work with each other. While we focus on students experiencing homelessness in this book, an ecology of promise has the potential to positively influence all at-promise student groups. These approaches to teaching and leadership are effective in many ways.

Norms for Engaging With Students

Educators who engage in proactive, holistic, developmental, and strengths-oriented practices have the potential to positively influence students' experiences and outcomes. These concepts are likely familiar to many educators; however, they are rarely presented as a comprehensive approach. When engaging with a student, an educator uses these norms as a checklist of sorts to reflect on how to approach a specific situation with a student and family as well as how to structure the classroom or other educational setting. These norms also guide how practices and policies are developed and implemented.

Proactive approaches involve educators regularly reaching out to students to build relationships, identify challenges, and connect students with opportunities. Educators get to know students, which enables them to recognize when the students may need additional forms of support. Instead of waiting for an issue to magnify, the goal is to proactively identify a concern and then leverage resources available to support the student. While students in elementary school may have one teacher who generally gets to know them well given the amount of time spent together, developing this kind of deep knowledge of students can be more challenging in middle and high school when students and families do not have one educator who serves as their point of contact. In these situations, students may feel disconnected. Proactive approaches involve educators communicating with each other to identify patterns and issues that may be emerging. School and district leadership need to design systems to facilitate these collaborative proactive approaches.

The proactive norm can look different depending upon the educators' role. For example, the front desk staff member ensures that all students and families fill out a residency questionnaire and assists them in understanding why this information is important. If a student falls within the category of homeless or housing insecure, the staff member then communicates this to their teacher, a counselor, and other relevant staff. Teachers proactively reach out to students and families to build relationships with them. This is especially important when they recognize that a student may be having challenges associated with attendance, social connections, or other issues. If a student is identified as homeless, the college preparation coordinator should reach out to them to provide information about college and the programming available. Transportation often creates a significant challenge for students; instead of waiting for students to miss class, educators can proactively create a transportation plan (and backup plan) with students (see Chapter 5). These are a few examples, but there are many more ways that educators can proactively connect with and support students experiencing homelessness.

Holistic approaches involve considering the student's background, personality, goals, academic experiences, and other important aspects of self when engaging with them and connecting them with resources. Students who attended many different schools may have a difficult time forming relationships with teachers and students because they do not expect to remain in one location. The student's personality will likely frame how they develop relationships and the amount of shame they feel about their housing situation. The student's background and characteristics may shape both their residential and educational experiences. Considering the student holistically enables educators to be more aware of how to support them in taking advantage of the services and opportunities that are available as well as when a challenge emerges.

When an issue emerges, educators take time to gather enough information to holistically understand what happened before addressing the situation. For example, a student may frequently arrive late to school, not have a proper uniform, or miss key homework assignments. The school policy may state that this student should receive detention or other consequences. In gathering information, it may be that the student is intentionally defying school policy and should be given consequences. However, there may be legitimate reasons for their behavior, for example:

- A student couch surfing may have inconsistent transportation to school.
- A student living in a shelter or storage room may not have the ability to wash clothes on a regular basis.
- A student living in a car may not have the space or resources needed for homework assignments.

These students may not openly discuss these issues, which is why the educator should proactively reach out to the student and have a conversation that considers the context before enforcing consequences. If the goal is to improve behavior and academic outcomes, a holistic approach may be more effective than strictly enforcing punishment, which may magnify the issue. For example, a student given a detention may not make it to the shelter in time to secure a bed for the night.

Developmental approaches involve considering the students' developmental stage and providing coordinated support throughout the students' educational journey. Teacher preparation programs often involve engaging with research and theory related to individual development. The mind and body develop from infancy through adolescence and the transition to adulthood. The traumas that an individual experiences can be magnified depending upon where they are in their developmental process. Educators, school sites, and districts can also work to create programming and support for students as they navigate schooling over time.

Students in elementary school may not have the language to express what is happening in their lives or how the situation impacts them. These young people may benefit from alternative approaches to expressing themselves and processing their emotions, such as art or play therapy. Younger children are not as independent and tend to be particularly vulnerable, which means that additional considerations may need to be made when providing support. For example, a 6-year-old who moves outside of the school boundaries would not be able to ride public transportation by themselves.

Some aspects of being homeless or housing insecurity magnify as the student gets older. Students in middle or high school may experience the challenges, including:

- Having inconsistent access to a shower, clean clothes, or personal care supplies, which may discourage their attendance and/or impact their peer relationships.

- Lacking a quiet space with the necessary resources (including access to the internet) needed to complete papers and projects.
- Meeting family expectations to assist with the care of siblings, which reduces the time they have for homework, activities, and sleep.

Educators working with these students should consider the context of how they navigate school. That is not to say that expectations should be lowered. Rather, educators can explore how to tailor support that recognizes the students' needs.

Strengths-oriented approaches involve considering the students' assets, talents, skills, previous successes, and personality traits that they bring to school with them—instead of primarily focusing on their assumed challenges or shortcomings. During initial interactions with students and families experiencing homelessness, educators may have a difficult time identifying strengths. Several challenges may be present, including limited finances, unstable housing, traumatic experiences, fragmented relationships, and low academic achievement—all of which may show up initially as behavioral issues.

An important aspect of using a strengths-oriented approach involves pausing to reflect on educators' assumptions. First, students have individual experiences. While there are overall patterns that help educators understand the potential challenges that may result from homelessness and housing insecurity, each student's experience differs. For example, a student living in a family shelter may have developed a community of support within that organization, or a student may have significant academic potential that does not easily show up in grades because they frequently move between schools. A strengths-oriented approach requires focusing on each student instead of making assumptions about students who are homeless.

Second, all students possess strengths—even if they may not be immediately evident. All the students we have worked with spoke about goals, aspirations, and passions. Some of the students had close relationships with parents, guardians, other family members, or community members. Students may have experienced academic success in the past before their housing instability interrupted their academic engagement. The students may also have taken leadership roles in their families or, for those disconnected, for themselves.

Third, approaching a student from a strengths orientation increases the educator's ability to build a trusting relationship with the student. In many cases, a student may have had several interactions with adults that began with an assumption that they are a problem, broken, with very little chance of achieving future stability and success. Each of these previous interactions then reinforces any negative beliefs that students hold of themselves. Approaching a student from a strengths orientation may also enable the student to shift how they perceive their potential. As they develop a trusting relationship with the educator, the student may be more likely to share their goals and aspirations. By drawing upon the proactive and holistic relationships that educators develop with students, they can identify the individual student's strengths and leverage them to support the student.

Norms for Engaging With Other Educators

How educators engage with each other also changes within an ecology of promise. To become an ecology, educators across the school and district need to agree on the norms and come together regularly to review their implementation. This requires collaborating with educators within and outside of the school site (including community partners) as well as engaging in reflective practice on how to continually improve programming and support provided for students.

Collaborative approaches involve building connections among teachers, staff, administrators, district leadership, state leaders, and community partners to create integrated and reinforcing positive experiences across the students' ecology of promise. Collaborative approaches enable educators to work together on a shared set of goals and to divide the work. Collaborative work also lets educators see where there may be duplicate, ineffective, or missing resources or supports. The comprehensive support that students experiencing homelessness often need will only be accomplished if collaboration occurs between educators within and across institutions.

Collaboration enables educators to gain a deeper understanding of the strengths, challenges, and resources that exist within different educator roles. Educators have different training, backgrounds, and perspectives that frame how they approach their work. Collaboration allows educators to leverage these different approaches and strengths. In addition, collaboration creates the context for educators to build trusting relationships and explore how to support the work of each individual educator. Educators who are part of a larger team often feel lower levels of burnout because they do not feel individually responsible for meeting the needs of each student.

Reflective approaches involve consistently considering how students, families, staff, and leadership experience the educational policies and practices, and being prepared to make changes to improve student success. This process leverages both formal data and practitioner experiences to inform decision-making and subsequent actions. Collective reflection enables educators to see different sides of an issue and may result in more effective solutions.

Site, district, and state leaders often need to create the context for educators to engage in reflective practice. The day-to-day workload and fresh, urgent challenges generally leave little time for educators to engage in reflection. The professional learning community activities provided with each chapter here encourage reflective practice. These tools could be used as they are or adapted to facilitate either individual or collective reflection.

CHAPTER CONCLUSION

Many policies and practices exist within schools and districts whose reason for being and history of development we seldom question. The ecology of promise approach lets educators revisit these often taken-for-granted aspects of school, district, and state operations to explore new ways of supporting students and families. When this is done collaboratively, educators can leverage each other's knowledge, experience, and creativity to revise policies and reimagine practices that undermine the educational engagement and success of students experiencing homelessness.

We should be clear: The norms within the ecology of promise do not mean that students should not have consequences for their actions. A student experiencing homelessness—like any student—may break a school or district policy. A consequence would likely be appropriate if the student intentionally disobeys important rules. Our overarching recommendation is to leverage the ecology of promise framework to gain a deeper understanding of the situation before determining the appropriate consequence.

Guiding Questions for Individual and/or Group Reflection

1. What would it look like to holistically support the students in your school or district who are experiencing homelessness? What services, resources, or services would be needed to make this possible? How could collaborative approaches among educators in different roles assist in this process?
2. Reflect on the term *at-promise* and how it shifts the way educators approach working with students experiencing homelessness. What would it look like to center each student's potential when engaging with them? What would it look like for schools and districts to fulfill their commitment to supporting students?
3. Consider how trauma-informed approaches could be integrated into your work. What policy or practice could be revised to provide trauma-informed support for your students?
4. What would it look like to create an ecology of promise in your classroom, school, district, or state?

Professional Learning Community Activities

Activity 1: Student Vignette

Review the student vignette in Appendix B. Then discuss the following questions:

1) Consider the ecology of promise norms related to supporting students—strengths-oriented, proactive, holistic and developmental.
    a) What evidence of these norms do you see in the vignette?
    b) Where might there have been opportunities to leverage the norms to provide additional support for Carlos?
2) Consider the ecology of promise norms related to educators working collaboratively and reflectively.
    a) How could educators (teachers, counselors, psychologist, special education services, ELL staff, extracurricular program advisors/ coaches, lunchroom staff, front office staff, and others) at your school site working with a student in a similar situation leverage these norms to provide support?
    b) How could district-, county-, and state-level educators be included within the planning and support process?
    c) How could community partners be incorporated into the planning and support of a student in a similar situation?
3) Can you think of a student or subgroup of students who live doubled-up?
    a) If you are unsure, how could you find out?
    b) If yes, what would it look like to create an ecology of promise for these students?

Activity 2: Utilizing Trauma-Informed Approaches

The Ohio Department of Education (n.d.) created action steps that move schools and districts toward trauma-informed services and away from bureaucratic compliance. These steps include:

- School districts reduce class sizes in classrooms with the highest mobility rates.
- Teachers or liaisons contact new families immediately to fully understand and appreciate families' circumstances and explain the options that are available for their child.
- Discuss the impact of school transfers with families, as well as what the school and family can do to help the student through the transition.
- Have information packets for families who enter after the beginning of the school year.
- Provide more detailed information in the school records of highly mobile students to allow future teachers to better determine academic and course enrollment options.
- Have a system for forwarding complete records to new schools or districts quickly. Provide packets to help families organize their student's academic records.

- Provide school brochures to local shelters to encourage children's attendance by providing parents with information about enrollment procedures and transportation.
- Provide opportunities for parents to meet with teachers and staff to share information about their child and to receive information about their child's progress in school.
- Discuss barriers faced by the family and help link the family to service providers.
- Provide tutoring, homework help, or credit recovery after school at the school building or at community locations to help students with their academic progress.
- Provide snacks or full meals.
- Ensure that at least one educator is committed to serving as a supportive, caring adult in the child's life while attending the school. This adult should connect with the child regularly.
- Coordinate services between the school, shelters, health care providers, and housing organizations to address needs of these families.
- Partner with community agencies to provide:
    - » Nutritious meals, including dinner for students who are in after-school activities;
    - » Storage space for personal belongings;
    - » Clothing solicited from apparel companies;
    - » Personal hygiene items and bathing facilities;
    - » Health services or clinic referrals; and
    - » Information on public assistance and services. (pp. 1–2)

Not all these steps can be accomplished perfectly or at the same time. Schools and districts interested in moving toward becoming trauma-informed providers of educational services would need to map out a plan for change. These practical steps provide a place to start.

- What trauma-informed practices and policies exist with your school/district? Are these done in pockets or across the school/district?
- What trauma-informed practices or polices could be integrated as a next step in supporting students? What resources are needed? Who would implement the practices? Who might need to give approval?
- How could a formal process be developed to review progress toward becoming a trauma-informed school or district?

Activity 3: Leveraging Ecology of Promise to Review Practices

Identify a school, districts, or state policy or practice that could be changed by the PLC members. Utilize the ecology of promise approach to review and adjust as needed. Develop a plan for adjustments and for continued reflection on policies and practices as the school, district, and/or state move toward creating an ecology of promise.

A few ideas to use as inspiration:

- Reflect on the formal and informal communications sent to students and families (e.g., written policies, student residency questionnaire, classroom newsletters, infraction documentation, resource sheets for students/families experiencing homelessness).. Review the documents through the ecology of promise lens. How could you change the language to be more proactive, strengths-oriented, holistic, and developmental?
- Identify a policy related to students experiencing homelessness. What is the underlying goal of the policy? How effective has the policy been in achieving that goal? Does the wording of the policy and implementation reflect an ecology of promise? If not, what adjustments to the policy or implementation of the policy could be made?
- Consider a current community partnership (or one that you would like to develop). How does the partnership reflect an ecology of promise? Are there ways to integrate the norms in new ways within the partnership?

Part II

EDUCATIONAL CONTEXT

CHAPTER 5

Evaluating and Implementing Policy

Federal, state, and local governments create and revise laws that serve to protect educational rights of marginalized students. Several decades ago, the federal government recognized the need to protect the educational rights of youth experiencing homelessness. Students with disabilities, as well as those experiencing poverty and housing instability, were previously denied educational rights. Accordingly, laws such as the Individuals with Disabilities Education Act (IDEA) and McKinney-Vento Act were developed to ensure that students' educational rights were not infringed upon. These policies have powerful implications for students and their families. Prior to the creation of these legal rights, many students were denied full access to a public education.

Some educators may be unaware of the federal mandates or financial resources available. In this chapter, we discuss federal policy that provides an expansive and inclusive definition of homelessness and frames how districts and schools serve students without residential stability. Further, we explore proposed legislative efforts to enhance current policies and those that expand educational access and protections for students experiencing residential instability.

OVERVIEW OF MCKINNEY-VENTO AND ESSA

School principals and teachers may be familiar with a district program that provides backpacks, school supplies, and transportation vouchers for students with financial need. There is a good chance this program originates from federal mandates concerning educational access for students experiencing homelessness. The McKinney-Vento Homeless Assistance Act, first passed in 1987, validates and articulates the educational rights of students experiencing homelessness by outlining several mandates that serve to increase educational access. Since 2001, the law has been expanded and revised several times, including in the most recent reauthorization of the 1965 Elementary and Secondary Education Act—the Every Student Succeeds Act (ESSA)—that was signed into law on December 10, 2015. ESSA covers a wide range of educational issues, including strengthening the supports for youth who are homeless that were outlined in the McKinney-Vento Act. While there may have been disagreement with the functionality and utility of the law as a broad policy for education, most agreed that the provisions related to student homelessness demonstrate a significant step forward in terms of educational access and success. Many schools, districts, and states improved data gathering as well as revised policies and practices to encourage the educational success of students based upon the federal guidance.

Due to the global pandemic of 2020, Congress approved the American Rescue Plan (ARP) Act, which set aside Elementary and Secondary School Emergency Relief (ESSER) funds to address the increased need for funding to provide support and resources to children and youth experiencing residential instability. This program allocated $24 million to Local Educational Agencies (LEAs), allowing them to better identify and support students experiencing residential instability. This funding reduced barriers to accessing educational programming. This effort was a short-term infusion of funding available for use from July 2021 through September 2024. Although this funding was short-term, several state coordinators and LEAs reported positive educational impact on meeting needs of students identified under McKinney-Vento. The National Center for Homeless Education (NCHE) published guidelines on their website—*American Rescue Plan-Homeless Children and Youth* (ARP-HCY)—that discussed how to use the funding, including a sustainability plan that promoted building staff capacity and developing fiscal partnerships for program longevity. While these funds have been expended, the sustainability plan can serve as a template for the development of fiscal partnerships and building of staff capacity.

National Center for Homeless Education (NCHE)

The National Center for Homeless Education (NCHE) offers support for families and educators who need guidance concerning providing support for students experiencing homelessness. The NCHE website (nche.ed.gov) includes numerous resources for educators and policymakers related to supporting the educational access and success of students experiencing homelessness. We highlight a few here but encourage you to explore their website.

NCHE publishes the names of McKinney-Vento coordinators for each state. Administrators and teachers can identify their state coordinator to learn more about how their state coordinates and implements McKinney-Vento locally. Schools and districts can also benefit from developing communication and relationships with their McKinney-Vento state coordinator to obtain guidance and support for approaches and partnerships that best meet the needs of students identified under McKinney-Vento.

NCHE provides national and state data going back to the 2005–2006 academic year. In addition to providing overall numbers of students experiencing homelessness, the state-level data are broken down into the types of homelessness experienced by students in each state. Each state's page also has the state coordinator's information and links to the state websites.

NCHE has a hotline and email address for educators who want to speak with a representative who knows about the legal protections provided by McKinney-Vento, ESSA and other federal laws. Assistance is available in both English and Spanish.

NCHE Hotline: 305-306-8495
Email: NCHE.helpline@safalpartners.com
Website: http://center.serve.org/nche/helpline.php

We primarily focus on McKinney-Vento as revised by ESSA. We organize this discussion to reflect the most current policies at the time of this 2nd edition publication. Educators and school leaders should continue to gather additional information about updates to the federal, state, and district policies (see the box above with NCHE and state coordinator information for two resources). Individuals responsible for operating these programs, including the state coordinator and district liaison, will want to review the original policy documents to learn more nuanced information about full implementation of the policies. The National Association for the Education of Homeless Children and Youth (NAEHCY) and SchoolHouse Connection consistently update their websites with policy interpretation and implementation documents. Appendix C provides a summary of the McKinney-Vento Act and ESSA. In the following sections, we provide an overview as well as the implications for education practice.

(RE)DEFINING HOMELESSNESS

McKinney-Vento outlines a more expansive definition of homelessness than educational leaders may be familiar with. The federal mandate considers most unstable living environments to fall within the definition of homelessness. McKinney-Vento defines any student without a "fixed, regular and adequate" nighttime residence as homeless. The terms *fixed, regular,* and *adequate* allow the law to cover a larger number of young people who lack a stable residence than more narrow definitions such as those used by HUD. These terms are important to unpack to fully understand how homelessness is defined:

- A *fixed* residence does not change from night to night and remains stationary.
- A *regular* residence can be used on a nightly basis.
- An *adequate* residence meets the physical and psychological needs that would be expected within a typical home environment.

- Also, *and* implies that students must have a residence that is fixed, regular, *and* adequate—if a student's residence does not meet all three of these criteria, then they fall under McKinney-Vento protections.

For example, if a student and their family temporarily stay with various family members or friends or reside in hotels/motels, this residence is not considered fixed or regular, as it is in constant flux. Further, students and families sleeping in cars, trains, or abandoned buildings lack adequate housing. If these conditions reflect a student's housing situation, then the student would be considered homeless under federal law and qualify for educational protection. The intersection of these three terms helps justify the inclusion of many forms of residential instability that go beyond common notions of homelessness. Many researchers and advocates have begun to use phrases like *housing insecurity, housing unstable,* and *highly mobile* to capture residential instability because it reflects the federal definition. This identifier may also be easier for youth and families to accept, since the label "homeless" tends to involve social shame.

Chapter 3 that youth who are homeless and highly mobile have multiple ways of enduring residential instability. The ways these young people experience homelessness directly impact how they access and engage the school system. Young persons living in a shelter often lack personal space to complete homework and may be required to follow strict rules. These shelter policies may impact how fully the student can participate in educational activities and supplemental programming. For example, a shelter with a curfew for residents could negatively impact involvement in sports or other extracurricular activities. Families in hotels also live in crowded conditions. They may feel a greater sense of personal freedom than those in shelters, but often have less access to regularly prepared meals or social service agency support. Young people living in a car, abandoned building, barn, or campsite often have uncomfortable sleeping conditions with limited structure that make getting to school on time or completing homework difficult. Students couch surfing often live between several friends and family members' houses, meaning that when they are in school, they are often preoccupied with trying to find a secure house to stay at each night. These students may have to travel a great distance each day to the school site because they are unable to control the location of their housing. Young people in transitional living units may have more space and structure, but the housing situation lasts only a few weeks or months. The fluidity of homelessness and highly mobile populations results in families and youth transitioning between many, if not all, of these different forms of residential instability. These youth may experience victimization, exploitation, and exposure to drugs, alcohol, and sexual activity.

The reauthorization of McKinney-Vento in 2001 as part of the No Child Left Behind Act expanded the definition of *homeless* to include those living doubled-up—,which involves multiple families/households living within a space designed for one family as a result of economic crises (see Chapter 3 for a full discussion of this and other forms of homelessness covered by federal law). The categorization as *doubled*-up is a bit of a misnomer, since there may be three or more families and individuals in one apartment or house. Although these students may have more structure to their lives and reduced likelihood of victimization, their living environment lacks stability. And the families in these doubled-up residences tend to be focused on finding ways to achieve an independent and stable household, which puts the arrangement at risk if one family or individual leaves. An unstable living environment like this is often a precursor to other forms of homelessness. Many educators and school staff are unaware that these students and families qualify for services provided by McKinney-Vento. In large part, this may be a result of the limited state and federal funding available for training school staff and educators about the intricacies of the law and how the mandates can be used to support students without housing stability.

Doubled-up families face several barriers in accessing federal protections and resources (Hallett, 2012a, 2012b). First off, many educators—as well as the families themselves—are unaware that these students qualify for services and support under McKinney-Vento federal law. School registration and attendance clerks may be suspicious of doubled-up families who attempt to use the federal protections or request resources. The training for front office staff may involve requiring all new students to show proof of residency and submission of paperwork before enrollment. Families without these materials may be perceived as trying to game the system. Some districts may also have student enrollment systems that allow for only one family to be assigned to each address, which makes it very difficult for doubled-up families to register for school. These students may be denied access to a free and appropriate public education if the federal provisions are not fully enacted.

Second, assuming a cultural preference to live with extended family can be tricky for school authorities. Without question, some families decide to invite friends or extended family members to live within the same residence for a myriad of mutually beneficial reasons. For example, grandparents move into the home to assist with raising young children, or older family members move into the home because they need assistance and can no longer live independently. A grandparent moving into a middle-class home with adequate space to accommodate all family members would not qualify as homeless. Understanding of what constitutes family within a particular home or community may differ amongst various racial/ethnic groups. Families may include extended family, longtime friends, and other important relationships. Cultural choices about who lives within a residence alone do not qualify a student as homeless under McKinney-Vento. Economic crises must also exist. For example, some of the families who prefer to live under one roof with extended family or friends may not be able to afford adequate space. If the housing involves inadequate space to support the number of people living within the dwelling, then they qualify for federal protections. As such, a student may live in a doubled-up residence for both cultural and economic reasons—which would mean that student qualifies for protections because of the economic conditions. When in doubt, educators should err on the side of assuming that the student qualifies for protections and then gather additional information later. The district homeless liaison or state coordinator can be a valuable resource when assessing the specifics of a student's situation.

The enduring economic challenges many communities face complicate the choices families make. Housing instability was exacerbated by the 2008 recession and by the COVID-19 pandemic, and many families are still trying to regain their footing due to loss of, or a significant reduction in, wages, coupled with a significant increase in housing costs across the country. Younger families, those who are most likely to have young children, have seen the sharpest drops in home ownership. In 1985, U.S. people ages 35–44 owned their home 68% of the time. By 2015, that percentage had fallen to 56% (Goodman & Mayer, 2018). Thus, almost half of families in prime child-rearing years are in the rental market or have arrangements other than home ownership. Many families who previously were able to secure and maintain stable, adequate housing are now facing homelessness. Moreover, while the eviction moratorium and subsequent funding provided by the federal government allowed residents to maintain their housing in order to shelter in place, the lost wages and accumulated back rent continue to place families at risk for eviction. Once a tenant is evicted, this (metaphorical) "Scarlet E" blemishes their housing record, making it even more difficult to secure housing (Desmond, 2017). This situation forces many families to move in temporarily with family or friends. Living doubled-up tends to be the first step when residential instability begins. As such, now more than ever, schools need to be aware of these precarious housing situations and ensure that students are being identified and provided the appropriate services under McKinney-Vento.

One note about definitions is worth mentioning. The federal government has different agencies that oversee education and housing. The Department of Education utilizes the McKinney-Vento definition of homelessness to determine which students and families are eligible for support. However, the Department of Housing and Urban Development (HUD) employs different definitional parameters when determining who is eligible for housing. Most notably, HUD excludes students and families living doubled-up. While HUD acknowledges the precarious living situations of doubled-up families, the consistent underfunding experienced by HUD limits its ability to support individuals and families living on the streets and in shelters. The decision has been made to enact a more conservative definition of homelessness until funding levels rise. Therefore, a student may be deemed in need of educational support as a result of being classified as homeless or highly mobile under McKinney-Vento but not qualify for housing support that would mediate the residential instability through HUD. This further complicates the process of informing individuals about their rights because they may be considered homeless by one federal service, but not another. In addition, it means that they may receive services specifically aimed at keeping them in school while not being eligible for support that would address the underlying issue—residential instability. Educators and advocates need to be aware of these conflicting qualifications to help students and families negotiate the confusion about their eligibility for educational support.

Educational Policy and Youth in Foster Care

McKinney-Vento previously included "awaiting foster care placement" within the definition of homelessness. Prior to ESSA, foster youth had few explicitly stated educational protections at the federal level. Youth awaiting foster care placement were removed from the definition of homelessness in ESSA. Advocates and policymakers determined that the educational needs of foster youth require specific consideration. As such, ESSA articulates protections for foster youth that are far more expansive than previous educational policies. Given the focus of this book, we are unable to provide a detailed discussion of those provisions or the implications. However, several policy organizations have begun releasing briefs to explain how to implement these protections, including the Alliance for Children's Rights and the Child Welfare Gateway. Most states and districts also have policies and resources specifically designed to support youth in or exiting foster care.

EDUCATIONAL ACCESS MANDATES

The federal government recognizes that being homeless negatively impacts access to school and, as a result, these students warrant special protections. McKinney-Vento and ESSA outline several mandates that states, districts, and schools must follow to qualify for grant funding associated with the law. To qualify for federal grant funding, each state must review all laws and policies to align with federal policy. To provide some clarity concerning the different aspects of how McKinney-Vento and ESSA frame the educational policies from the state to site levels, we discuss the tenets of each organizational level.

State Level

As with all students, youth and families experiencing homelessness must have equal access to free and appropriate public education. This mandate extends from preschool through high school graduation and includes supplemental educational support and alternative school arrangements that may be needed for the student to fully access the curriculum. State-level educational organizations must carefully review all policies to ensure none of them impede access for students without residential stability. Policies that create barriers must be changed. For example, states with a compulsory local residency requirement for school attendance are required to review provisions to ensure they align with federal mandates. These requirements cannot violate the McKinney-Vento and ESSA mandates that enable students experiencing homelessness to remain at school of origin even if they move outside of the geographic boundaries.

States receive money to support the implementation of McKinney-Vento and ESSA. Each state determines how McKinney-Vento funds will be distributed to school districts. Funding for the 2024–2025 school year was $129 million, an amount that remains unchanged from 2024. Often, districts are required to submit grant proposals that outline the local need and how funding will be used. Approximately 20% of school districts receive McKinney-Vento funds (SchoolHouse Connection, 2025). Districts outline how they will utilize the funding to support educational access and success of students experiencing homelessness. In some cases, a district may need funding to update their student residency tracking systems and provide training for educators related to identification to gain a more accurate picture of how many students experience homelessness. This can be particularly important for identifying students living doubled-up, which tends to be an invisible subgroup (Hallett, 2015b).

Each state is required to have a clearly defined process for overseeing how districts and sites implement McKinney-Vento. Each state is required to have a state coordinator to oversee their Education for Homeless Children and Youth (EHCY) program. These duties include (a) developing and implementing a state plan, (b) collecting, sharing, and disseminating data on students experiencing homelessness, (c) coordinating activities, (d) providing technical assistance, and (e) responding to inquiries from students, families, and unaccompanied youth (NCHE, 2023). Youth and families who disagree with how federal mandates have been judged to apply (or not) in their situation also need a way to challenge how services and resources have been distributed. The state should ensure that districts and sites provide families with information about filing a grievance. ESSA mandates that school of origin determination policy must involve a written letter to the parent, guardian, or youth (if unaccompanied) explaining why a student was denied the request to enroll at the specific school requested. The individuals filing the request should be given information about how to file an appeal with the state to review the case if they feel an error was made. These communications need to be written in a way that is accessible. A form letter with complicated jargon would not fulfill this mandate. The processes and individual rights need to be clearly understandable by the person who submitted the petition.

New Homeless Education State Coordinators

State coordinators play an essential role in developing a statewide plan and overseeing the implementation of services for students experiencing homelessness. The role involves managing funding, training educators, overseeing data, and working directly with students and families when the school site or district need assistance. Given the complexity of the role, we recruited a state coordinator to provide advice—see Appendix D.

District Level

Districts translate federal and state policies into processes that are to be implemented at the site level. As with other educational issues, districts determine how this policy fits within the mission and integrate the mandates within the district policies and procedures. As a general provision, the district must review all policies to determine how they may influence educational access for students who are homeless. Any policy that hinders the educational pursuits of youth and families without residential stability needs to be adjusted. McKinney-Vento and ESSA then articulate specific policies that should be considered. The remainder of this section provides an overview of those policies.

Students may choose to remain at their school of origin for as long they experience homelessness. This mandate recognizes the negative educational and social impacts when students lack school stability. Although students may move outside of the school boundaries, the district is required to provide transportation to the school of origin. This can be in the form of busing, gas cards, bus tokens, or other forms of transportation. Feasibility and what is in the best interest of the student also factor into the decision about mode of transportation. For example, a district would likely not want to require a 1st-grader to take multiple city buses to get to school each day. Students and families may determine that transferring to a local school near their new residence works better than remaining at the school of origin, but the district cannot mandate a transfer or make the process of staying at the school of origin overly laborious. If a parent or guardian requests to have the student transferred to a school site closer to their new living arrangement, the district should collaborate with the site of origin and the new site to ensure that the transfer occurs without delay. If a student regains residential stability, they have the right to remain at the school of origin until the end of the school year.

ESSA expanded this mandate to include preschool and feeder schools. The school of origin mandate does not end once the student has completed all the grade levels at that school site. The student can remain within the school feeder pattern until residential stability is established. For example, a student at an elementary school who remains homeless can transition to the middle school that elementary school feeds into, and the district must provide transportation for students to the school of origin and the feeder schools that become the student's new school of origin as they progress through the grade levels. Providing transportation to fulfill this mandate has been difficult for many schools and districts. We worked with one school district for which transporting students who are homeless involves transportation across state lines and figured out how to split costs between districts. Unfortunately, many school districts remain out of compliance with the transportation mandate—which was also part of McKinney-Vento—due to the significant cost associated with students who end up in distant locations. This puts the school and district at risk of lawsuits.

ESSA makes the students' residential situation part of their educational record. As such, the classification as homeless is protected by Family Educational Rights and Privacy Act (FERPA). The designation of homeless should not be shared with anyone outside of the school. Even within the school and district, only those individuals who need to know about the students' residential classification should have access to the information.

The district, in coordination with the state, needs to ensure that liaisons have access to professional development related to McKinney-Vento and ESSA. The training should include how to appropriately identify and support students. In addition, the liaisons need to be given training whenever policy updates occur. It is recommended that districts and schools provide at minimum annual training for all school personnel to ensure awareness and compliance with McKinney-Vento. Additionally, incorporating "refreshers" throughout the school year within professional development activities as well as prior to the start of the school year will increase understanding of and consistent implementation of McKinney-Vento requirements. Importantly, this will assist in the identification and connection to appropriate services to reduce barriers to educational access for students experiencing residential instability.

Districts receiving Title I funds need to set aside a portion of funding for students who are homeless. One exception exists to this requirement: It is waived if the district has no students experiencing homelessness. However, districts claiming zero covered students need to conduct a self-study to ensure that steps have been taken to thoroughly review whether students without residential stability have been correctly identified; districts receiving Title I funding are very likely to be serving students who lack residential stability. Districts that cannot show they are exempt must determine what portion of the Title I funding they receive will be designated for students experiencing homelessness. Generally speaking, four different approaches exist: (1) the homeless liaison determining a reasonable amount needed to meet the educational needs of students who are homeless in the district; (2) multiplying the number of students who are homeless identified by the district's Title I, Part A per pupil allocation; (3) matching the amount of McKinney-Vento subgrant funding received; or

(4) reserving a percentage based upon the district's poverty level. This funding cannot be used to pay for services required by McKinney-Vento; the money is meant to ensure that students experiencing homelessness at non-Title I schools have access to the same supplemental programming they would receive at Title I schools. For example, Title I funds cannot be used for transportation to school; however, they could be used to provide transportation to activities outside of the school day or to assist parents who wish to attend school events.

Each district is required to identify a homeless liaison to facilitate the implementation of McKinney-Vento and ESSA mandates. The district should provide appropriate training for the liaison. This person becomes the point of contact for school sites and families who need assistance in accessing services and resources. The liaison is responsible for ensuring that the school sites and district comply with federal law and state policies concerning students experiencing homelessness. As a best practice, many districts now also require that a point of contact be identified at each school site who will collaborate with the district liaison. Frequently, the point of contact is a guidance counselor, social worker, attendance coordinator, or assistant principal.

The district, often via the oversight of the homeless liaison, works in collaboration with school sites and community organizations to provide any supplies that may be required to attend school, but may be inaccessible to students because of their homeless situation. This includes backpacks and school uniforms that may be financially inaccessible, but necessary. Also, school supplies that may be needed to complete homework or those that teachers ask families to donate to the classroom should be provided for the student. The district can either purchase these supplies or work in collaboration with community organizations to ensure that students gain access to these materials.

School districts must ensure that students experiencing homelessness and high rates of mobility are not segregated based upon their residential status. For example, a school for students who are homeless located in a shelter would be a clear violation of federal law. Advocates fought to disallow segregated schools after numerous sites were found to have uncredentialed teachers, poor facilities, and inadequate educational materials. In addition, isolating youth experiencing homelessness from their peers was found to negatively impact their social development. While providing specialized support to youth in homeless situations in one location may sound like a good idea, the implementation frequently resulted in subpar educational environments and limited exposure to housed peers. For example, some youth living in homeless shelters would attend class in a small room within the shelter with a teacher's aide running the curriculum. (A few districts have schools for students experiencing homelessness that existed prior to the federal mandate and have been allowed to continue to operate under careful oversight by the district and state.)

Students who are homeless may attend alternative schools or programs based upon educational needs, but these must be the same schools that serve the overall population of the district and not be specifically designed for those who are experiencing homelessness. A student cannot be placed in these programs simply due to their housing status. School districts may design transitional schools or programs that help facilitate access for students who are highly mobile and lack residential stability. However, these transitional sites should not become permanent placements. For example, the Bethune Center in Long Beach, California, offers a short-term transitional school for students in kindergarten through 8th grade. The student experiencing homelessness who has been out of school for some time can attend the center for a week or two while educational assessments are conducted, and an educational transition plan can be created. Transitional schools tend to be more difficult for high school students because they need to be enrolled immediately to continue accruing credits toward graduation. ESSA does include provisions to ensure that students get partial credit when they complete some coursework at one high school and transfer to another.

While not a required mandate, it is recommended that districts have a school board–approved policy that outlines how students and families experiencing homelessness and high mobility are served. We encourage school boards to engage in conversations about how supporting these students fits within their vision and mission.

Site Level

As with the state and district institutional levels, school sites have the general mandate to review all policies to determine if any inhibit educational access for homeless youth. This review process should include all aspects of schooling, including the administrative procedures, support services, classroom activities, and extracurricular opportunities. All barriers restricting full educational access for students should be removed. A good rule of thumb is that students should have access to the same educational opportunities as their stably housed peers. Increasing student access will likely also include providing consistent training for all school staff and personnel.

McKinney-Vento also outlines specific mandates for school sites. Students identified as homeless must be allowed to enroll immediately. Most schools and districts have policies requiring immunization records, transcripts, and other required documents before enrollment can be completed. Students experiencing homelessness may endure several different school placements within one year—particularly if they move around the state or nation. The unstable lifestyle could result in misplaced documents as families and students are forced to leave things behind when they suddenly make a residential transition. Schools may also not be aware that a student has moved, which could delay the transition of information to the new school. Waiting for cumulative files to be located and transferred between schools or districts can take days or weeks. To avoid having students without residential stability missing several school days each time they move, the school is required to enroll these students and allow them to attend while the necessary documents are being located.

Schools may not require proof of residency from students and families who are homeless. A tenuous living situation can make such documentation difficult or impossible to secure. For example, families living doubled-up may not have rental agreements or utility bills in their name. Similarly, youth living in cars or couch surfing may not have a stable geographic location that would allow for residential documentation. And emergency shelters do not allow individuals to claim permanent residence. Students are identified as homeless because they do not have a stable residence; a mandate for proof of residency would result in these students being denied access to education. Sending out residency verification mailings would also be a violation. We have observed schools that send a letter to all students a few weeks into the school year. Any "return to sender" letters received by the school are used to drop enrollment of students until a parent or guardian can prove local residency. For students experiencing homelessness, this would violate McKinney-Vento. Even for those not previously identified as homeless, the "return to sender" mailings should raise a red flag that something may have happened to the family. Instead of using this to exclude students from schools, it should be part of a conversation to figure out what is happening and then decide the appropriate next steps. Another approach would be to develop internal documentation that would allow a family to document their temporary residence. For example, in Louisiana, schools can complete a Student Residency Questionnaire that is aligned with the definition of homelessness outlined in McKinney-Vento. This form allows families and unaccompanied students to identify their housing situation as well as capture other services or needs such as school supplies and IDEA support. We would encourage having practices in place that limit educational disruption until a determination is made that the student does not qualify for protections under McKinney-Vento.

Unaccompanied homeless youth are permitted to enroll without a legal guardian present. This subpopulation of homeless youth lacks connection to a parent, guardian, or social service agency. (Couch surfers, for example, transition between the residences of friends and family without connection to a guardian.) After the student has been enrolled, the school administrator or counselor can reach out to family and social service agencies—depending on what is most appropriate given the specific student's situation—to identify emergency contact persons and other important information. It is critical to understand the youth's situation prior to making contact with the family, as many unaccompanied youth experience homelessness due to family conflict and therefore contacting the family could place the youth at risk for harm.

Schools must facilitate access for students in homeless situations to all programs and services that are available to the general student population. These include programs offered during the school day as well as after-school programming and activities. ESSA explicitly expanded the law to cover summer school, co-curricular activities, and preschool. The complex social contexts that frame these young people's lives mean that they may need access to migrant or special education services. With rare exceptions, students experiencing homelessness qualify for free breakfast and lunch programs; they may need some assistance filling out the required forms.

ROLE OF THE HOMELESS LIAISON

The district homeless liaison serves as an important link between the state, district, and school sites and is the primary facilitator of McKinney-Vento and ESSA mandates within the district. Often, this person is located with the district office and may have multiple other responsibilities. Many county offices of education will also have a designated administrator who oversees the districts and can assist with providing training for the district liaisons.

Federal and state laws provide specific guidance concerning the roles of homeless liaisons. First, they are responsible for overseeing the identification process for students who are homeless. This involves making sure a specific process for coding homelessness exists when students enroll in school. School sites need to be able to designate that students qualify for McKinney-Vento during the registration process as well as if residential instability occurs at any point in time during the school year. Many schools use some form of residency questionnaire that enables parents or guardians to denote that they qualify for McKinney-Vento. While many schools collect this information at the beginning of the school year and when students register as new students, we recommend gathering this information at several points throughout the year. The residential situations of students experiencing homelessness may change frequently throughout the school year. In addition, students with previously secure housing may lose stability in the middle of the year and not know that resources exist. Given the importance of addressing challenges early to limit impact on educational performance, school sites and districts should consider when they could gather residential updates from all students throughout the year (e.g., quarterly grading periods, parent conferences, beginning of semesters).

Directly asking if a student is homeless generally does not yield accurate results because students may not fully understand the various living arrangements that qualify. The homeless liaison also provides training for administrative assistants in the school site offices to ensure that they understand how the identification process works and why it is important to correctly identify students. Teachers and other staff at the school also need training to recognize need and provide the appropriate connections for a student who may need services. In many districts, the homeless liaison will conduct training for the front office staff and new teachers each fall to ensure that they understand how the processes work and why they are important. Some districts also require that each school site identify a homeless designee—often this is a counselor, social worker, attendance coordinator, or assistant principal. The homeless liaison would also provide training for these individuals. While having designees at each site may not be required by law, we have found that this helps facilitate the full implementation of the federal mandates within the local context. In addition, having a site-based designee gives school staff, students, and family members a point of contact within the school.

The homeless liaison also coordinates referrals for supplemental services (e.g., for mental or physical health) that may be needed to support students' full participation in school. In addition, they work with Head Start and preschool programming to ensure that students experiencing homelessness have access to these services. Since many students and families experiencing homelessness are unaware of their rights, the homeless liaison provides training and support to allow students and families to take full advantage of educational opportunities and support. The liaison should post public notices that outline the educational rights of students who are homeless and highly mobile. While posting a flier in the school office may meet the letter of the law for McKinney-Vento, liaisons should implement more active and effective strategies to inform students and parents of their rights. Given the continuing development and rise in technology and social media, in addition to posting physical information documents at the school site, learning management systems and popular platforms such as Facebook and Instagram can be vehicles of resource dissemination and information collection. ESSA pushes districts and school sites to more actively share information with students and families to ensure that they know their rights and how to gain access to resources. As disputes concerning access to education and services arise, the liaison takes steps to resolve parent and student concerns.

Even in districts with a large proportion of students identified as homeless, the liaison may also be tasked with significant other responsibilities. Ingram and colleagues (2016) found that approximately 90% of liaisons had significant other responsibilities and job titles and could designate only half or less of their time to their role as homeless liaison. In some places, individuals have so many roles that they are not even aware they are the designated liaison for their school. This often occurs because of the limited funding available to support the liaison in taking time to connect students to resources as well as attending training to learn more about the role and its requirements. We encountered a district that had selected the Child Welfare and Attendance Coordinator as the homeless liaison, which meant that this individual held several other district coordinator roles, including the school police, attendance and student attendance review board (SARB), alternative schools, adjudicated youth, foster youth, and pregnant and parenting students. Even though over 15% of students were identified as homeless in the district, the liaison was able to dedicate only a modest amount of time to that role. The Government Accountability Office (2014) found that homeless liaisons spend approximately 2 hours per day dedicated to that role because of the numerous other responsibilities associated with juggling multiple other roles. In some districts, an upper-level administrator may be assigned the designation as the homeless liaison, but a few full-time assistants are hired to implement the mandates under the supervision of the liaison. This structure can also be a way to increase the staffing to serve students experiencing homelessness as well as the schools they attend. ESSA now explicitly requires that the person chosen as the liaison "must be able to carry out their duties described in the law." For many districts, this may mean assessing whether adjustments need to be made to free up the homeless liaison's time to implement the McKinney-Vento and ESSA mandates. While we appreciate that districts are under financial constraints, we encourage reviewing the ability of homeless liaisons to adequately fulfill the federal and state mandates when expected to also fulfill numerous other responsibilities. This is not only best practice but also protects the district from future litigation.

Homeless liaisons typically coordinate the review of transportation, identification, enrollment, and other policies at the district level to identify and remove barriers. They also provide training for school sites and support educators who have questions about how to support students identified as homeless. In addition, this individual often works directly with homeless families and unaccompanied youth to ensure they understand their rights and gain access to necessary resources and services. At times, families or students will be referred directly to the homeless liaison when the school site needs additional help meeting their needs. The student's needs may also come to the attention of the liaison when a student, parent, or advocate files a complaint about lack of access to federally mandated services. Complaints about noncompliance from families and students are, however, infrequent because of the shame associated with identifying as homeless coupled with the lack of awareness concerning the federal mandates. In addition, disagreements about school placement, transportation methods, and eligibility for services often get slowed by state appeal processes that are confusing and time-consuming. Ideally, homeless liaisons would have dedicated time to coordinate services at the school level and to cultivate relationships with community organizations, hospitals, and other resources that would address the out-of-school factors that are beyond what schools can provide. These partnerships will be further discussed in Chapter 9.

ROLES OF OTHER STAFF AND PROFESSIONALS

McKinney-Vento and ESSA do not directly identify the role of other staff and professionals at the school sites. However, the districts and sites are required to review all policies that may impede the full educational access of students experiencing homelessness. This places some of the responsibility on others within the district and site to be aware of the legal mandates and consider whether they are enforcing policies that may be impeding educational access, or worse, violating students' educational rights. For example, a school nurse cannot block enrollment because an immunization record has not been submitted. While not all educators and staff at the school site need to know which students are homeless, everyone should know about the federal mandates and who to contact if a student needs more information or additional support.

Researchers have found that school counselors and school social workers play an important role in facilitating access to McKinney-Vento protections (Baggerly & Borkowski, 2004; Havlik & Bryan, 2015). Counselors and social workers often have conversations with students and families about the challenges they are facing. The counselor or social worker may be the first person at the school to whom the student or family reveals their residential instability. They may form trusting relationships with the student and family, which can be used to share information about educational rights and resources. However, counselors and social workers have inconsistent knowledge about the rights of students experiencing homelessness. Again, here we want to reiterate that increasing awareness and understanding of McKinney-Vento for all school staff and personnel is instrumental to successfully supporting all students and families experiencing homelessness and housing insecurity.

ADHERENCE TO LEGAL REQUIREMENTS

While we believe that most educational leaders seek to implement McKinney-Vento and ESSA to support positive educational outcomes for students in homeless situations, we also need to acknowledge the potential legal ramifications for not complying with the federal mandates. As students, parents, and advocates become more aware of their rights, it becomes more likely that a district will face lawsuits if it does not protect educational access. Several states have already faced litigation, including Alabama, Hawaii, Maryland, and Illinois. The cases differ in terms of specifics, but all involve school personnel allegedly knowing students were homeless and not providing full access to the federal provisions. With the expansion of rights under ESSA as well as the push to ensure that students and families know their rights, districts need to be diligent about the implementation of the federal mandates. Ultimately, McKinney-Vento provides protections for students, families and schools. When well-implemented, schools can become collaborative spaces of community where students, no matter their housing status, thrive academically, developmentally, and socially.

CHAPTER CONCLUSION

Federal and state governments recognize the significant negative impact that homelessness can have on the educational process. The guidelines provided in federal law, in particular McKinney-Vento and ESSA, lay the foundations for policy and programming interventions. Implementing these mandates within the local context requires careful consideration of how the district and school sites can adjust policies to ensure that students experiencing homelessness have full access to their educational rights.

Guiding Questions for Individual and/or Group Reflection

1. How many students in your district or school site have been identified as homeless? Given McKinney-Vento's inclusive definition, do these numbers seem to reflect your student population? If not, what steps need to be taken?
2. How much funding has your state, district, and/or school received? How is that funding being used? Does it meet the needs of students and families? How do you know? Does your school have a sustainability plan in place?
3. How does federal policy differ from how people in your school or district define homelessness? How does the McKinney-Vento definition of homelessness inform services schools should provide to students and families?
4. What barriers exist at the district or site levels that inhibit students from fully accessing school or educational resources? What steps can be taken to resolve these issues?
5. What services are provided at the district and site levels? Are there community organizations that may provide supplemental support? What additional services may be needed?

Professional Learning Community Activities

Activity 1: Case Study of Family Experiencing Residential Mobility

Appendix E has a short vignette of a single mother navigating residential instability while attempting to encourage her children's educational engagement. The vignette includes embedded questions to guide reflection. Consider leveraging the ecology of promise approach when engaging with the vignette.

Activity 2: Strategies Related to Transportation

Providing consistent transportation to and from school for students experiencing homelessness can be one of the most difficult federal mandates to implement. Appendix F includes an overview of strategies one school district found effective. After reviewing the information, consider the following:

- How do students experiencing homelessness in your school or district get to school?
- Do you know of any students or families who have difficulty with transportation? Are there students who have stopped coming to school because they have inconsistent transportation?
- What policies or practices could be revised to create consistent transportation for all students experiencing homelessness in your school or district?
- How could transportation staff leverage the ecology of promise norms when developing and implementing these services?

Activity 3: Determining Student Residency Status

Schools and districts need to determine which students qualify as homeless under the McKinney-Vento Act. Many times, a Student Residency Questionnaire (SRQ) is used to gather information about a student's residency status. How the SRQ is designed and utilized can have a significant impact on if a school, district, and/or state has accurate data. In addition, the SRQ identifies students who are eligible for protections and supports.

- What process is used to identify students experiencing homelessness?
- If a SRQ is used, review the document to see if it reflects the ecology of promise norms and the multiple categories for homelessness protected by McKinney-Vento.
- Consider reviewing SRQs from other districts and states, especially if you currently do not use one. Most districts and states publish their SRQ online along with an explanation of the process used to distribute the forms.
- When is the SRQ distributed? How does the person administrating the SRQ explain the form and why it is important? If the form is distributed at enrollment, how do educators capture residency status changes throughout the academic year?
- After a student is identified, what happens next? Review the process using the ecology of promise norms. Are there adjustments that could be made to improve the support provided to students and families?
- How often are data reviewed by the school, district, or state? Are there additional ways the data could be incorporated into professional development and decision-making?

CHAPTER 6

Understanding the Context of Homelessness

Homelessness in the United States tends to be misunderstood. Many people hold to stereotypical notions, picturing an older person on the street who may struggle with substance abuse and mental illness. Communities need to find support for these individuals; however, this demographic may have little direct connection to educational leaders. As such, the topic may seem irrelevant for K–12 school districts and sites. In fact, persons who face homelessness in the United States come from a wide range of demographic categories and have complex life stories that lead up to their homelessness. Most of these people live in a family group. Their residential instability comes in many forms, including living in cars, hotels, or shelters. Some families seek shelter in abandoned buildings; a subset of unaccompanied youth couch surf. Further, under the McKinney-Vento Act, homelessness, in the context of educational institutions, applies to youth living doubled-up with another family (or more) because of economic crises (see Chapter 5). Turbulent economic times over the past several decades have resulted in an increase in families seeking refuge in doubled-up residences, and this is by far the largest subgroup of homeless students.

The relative invisibility of youth experiencing homelessness and high rates of mobility often results in limited educational support. Drawing from research and practice, this chapter explains how the context of homelessness influences how students engage with school. Making these young people visible to the district and school site is often the first step to adequately serving them. Clearly understanding the various forms of homelessness can assist educational leaders in developing tracking systems that more fully reflect the scope of homelessness in the district. We worked with a district that went from identifying 20 homeless students to almost 2,000 after investigating the federal law and reconfiguring student-tracking systems that enabled identification of all subcategories of homelessness discussed in the previous chapter (Hallett et al., 2015b).

Shame permeates the lives of students and families who are homeless and highly mobile. Taken-for-granted life experiences (e.g., bathing and sleeping) become further complicated with residential instability. Societal and social pressures create a sense of shame that can be debilitating for young people. Feeling different, unsafe, and "less than" can lead to individuals hiding from peers, teachers, social workers, and others. While this may be done to protect ego, it can severely limit a person's ability to take advantage of resources. Individuals in helping professions need to be keenly aware of protecting students' self-esteem while also creating safe spaces and programming that enable young people and their families to access vital support and resources.

COMPLEXITY OF STUDENT HOMELESSNESS

Adolescence tends to be a difficult time of self- and social acceptance. Individuals' bodies experience numerous changes that lead to complicated emotions and uncertain senses of self. These young people rely on others, specifically peers and family, to navigate the transition to adulthood. Being accepted by peers includes feeling valuable, attractive, intelligent, and safe. Shame may lead an individual to isolate or present a false self, both of which have unhealthy ramifications. In worst cases, shame can lead to destructive behaviors or actions. We have encountered teenagers who would avoid going to school because they did not have access to a shower or other forms of hygiene. One student spoke about how he lost a significant amount of weight while living on the streets and felt ashamed when students or teachers commented about his appearance. He went from having the athletic frame of a football player to being embarrassed to change in the locker room because other students would joke about seeing his ribs. The lack of residential stability creates significant shame for youth and has implications on other aspects of their educational life. For example, one elementary student explained how she did not turn in her math assignment because her teacher had asked all the students to draw a picture of her bedroom with measurements. Living in a shelter made this assignment embarrassing, if not impossible. The student could not bring herself to draw a shelter bedroom and present that to her classmates.

While common notions of homelessness presume low-income backgrounds, residential instability involves the intersection of many different social issues that can impact middle class as well as low income youth. For example, young persons who are kicked out of family homes or mothers with children fleeing domestic violence situations can come from communities of every financial level. The Great Recession demonstrated the fragility of the American economic situation and shook perceptions of residential security. Some middle-class communities witnessed several families moving into doubled-up residences as a result of the financial crises. These families wanted to stay within the school district where they previously owned a home so their children could continue to experience consistent and high-quality educational programming. Additionally, increasingly frequent, large-scale disasters such as hurricanes and wildfires can and do render entire communities (in the full range of economic circumstances) homeless in a matter of hours or days.

UNPLANNED MOBILITY

Youth categorized as homeless and highly mobile often are not the only students in the school or district who move between schools. School sites near a military base may have a significant portion of students who transfer in and out each year. Similarly, districts may serve communities with businesses that transfer employees around the country or world. Districts with a large number of agricultural jobs may experience seasonal mobility among their families. For any number of reasons, a school or district may become accustomed to a high rate of student turnover. While these situations will shape the students' educational history, they differ significantly from the mobility associated with homelessness.

Planned movement enables the family and school to prepare the student for a major life transition. Families in the military or who move for work often have some level of notice. Even if only given a couple of weeks, the family can plan for uprooting and moving to another location. The movement typically involves going from one stable home to another. The movement tends to occur infrequently—maybe once every few years. The family and student can work with the existing school to gather school records and set up as smooth a transition as possible to the next school. Families may even choose to leave one parent with the child to finish out the school year while another moves to the new location and begins getting their home settled. Planned movement, even if not desirable to the child, allows for time to psychologically prepare the young person for a new environment and community. The residential and educational move can be disruptive to relationships and schooling, but there tends to be some level of preparation and support for the child to minimize the potential negative educational and psychological impacts.

Unplanned mobility influences students differently from planned movement. A parent may find out in the afternoon that they can no longer stay at the shelter, or they may be kicked out of an abandoned building during the middle of the night. For those living doubled-up, a conflict may arise between families occupying a single home that forces an immediate departure from the residence, or a landlord may decide to evict all the families because there are more people in the apartment than stated on the lease. Individuals who experience homelessness live with a constant sense of instability. The more unplanned moves children experience, the less likely they may be to establish meaningful and long-term relationships (Fantuzzo et al., 2012; Tierney & Hallett, 2012). The structure of a stable home environment is absent, which changes how young people think about where they belong and where they feel safe. Whereas a planned move involves preparation, unplanned moves happen without much forethought or preparation. Families and students may feel the need to prioritize immediate basic needs while also trying to figure out how to continue accessing school. Unplanned moves and unexpected homelessness for families are on the increase in the United States. Following the pandemic that began in 2020, escalating rent prices have pushed more families over the line of spending more than 50% of household income on housing, widely considered to be a danger zone for housing instability (Kaysen, 2024). Additionally, nearly half of renter households in 2024 were considered *cost-burdened*, spending more than 30% of income on rent. There are also differences across racial groups—for example, Black families average 56% of income going to rent (U.S. Census Bureau, 2024).

Unplanned mobility impacts educational participation. A planned move, particularly when it occurs during the school year, often involves working with the teacher and school to gather student data that will be given to the next school. The class may have a small party or give the student a card to help celebrate this transition and to express how much the student was appreciated. Unplanned moves often happen without engaging the school. The student simply stops coming to class. This can be stressful for the student, teacher, and classmates. Students feel disconnected from educational institutions as they are funneled in and out of schools without much planning or follow-up. Additionally, the teachers, other school staff, and classmates may feel uncertain about when or if the student will return. An individual whom they have come to know has simply disappeared.

Unplanned movement for youth without residential stability may happen multiple times within one school year or even within one month. Instability may become the one constant in the lives of these young people. Latisha, a 17-year-old living in a family shelter, explained that being homeless "gives you more barriers, because instead of worrying about school, you worry about your life, you worry about what you're gonna do the next morning, when you go home, how are you gonna live, how you gonna sleep, how you gonna eat, how you gonna survive?" Students who have experienced several unplanned moves may be preoccupied with where they will sleep that night while they try to remain focused on the lesson in class and to find a place and time to complete their homework.

Many students with unplanned mobility often move within the same geographic region, which means they may end up in another school that is in the same district, county, or state. The student may also return to the school of origin in a few days, weeks, months, or years. District-, county-, and state-level institutions can play an important role in identifying these students and figuring out how to coordinate education support. For example, a teacher at the new school could be given access to the student's educational records and the previous teacher could share insights based upon their experiences with the student. If the school of origin is within a reasonable distance, the district or county could coordinate transportation back to that school even if the student is out of the attendance boundary area (a practice that is federally mandated—see Chapter 5). Educational institutions can also reach out to the student and family to explore how to coordinate support to reduce unplanned mobility or, at the very least, assist them in remaining engaged with school even if movement continues.

PARENTING WHILE HOMELESS

Some forms of homelessness force parenting into public spaces where other individuals scrutinize each decision that these parents or guardians make. Those in shelters constantly have staff, social workers, volunteers, and other residents offering feedback and critiquing expressions of affection, discipline, and family organization. Families living on the streets or in cars have those passing by watching and judging decisions about childrearing. Living in a doubled-up residence means a parent has at least one other family unit watching how choices are made; this may confuse children who see different family arrangements and disciplinary approaches bumping up against each other within the same dwelling. Parents in all these situations speak about feeling judged by the public for not providing better living arrangements for their children.

While having advice from trusted advisors can be helpful and the existence of other parenting units within a residence may allow for shared responsibility, most parents find that the lack of privacy creates tremendous stress. Most parents in residentially stable arrangements would admit that they have made mistakes. Examples of such mistakes might include allowing a child to get away with a small infraction because the parent is tired or speaking in a louder voice than one would have hoped because an action of the child scared the parent. In a private residence, a parent may reflect on the event and decide about how to proceed in the future. Homelessness magnifies the guilt and fear associated with these events, while the added stress of residential instability may limit the emotional availability of the parent. Not only does the parent need to be concerned about resolving the issue with the child, but the parent must make sure that others who are watching do not exaggerate the event and report them to social services. Many parents experiencing homelessness fear that educators and social workers will take their children because of the limited resources of the parent. This fear encourages parents and children to hide their need from those who might be able to assist.

At times, the overall stress of meeting basic needs of the family can be so overwhelming that little time and energy remains for parenting. This can be misunderstood as parents not caring about their children. Local or state authorities' initial reaction may be to find ways to remove the child from the care of the parent, instead of finding ways to meet the needs of the family in order to allow the individual to parent in a safe and supportive space. (Legally, homelessness alone cannot be used as a reason to remove a child from the parent's care and place them in foster care.)

An additional pressure that the growing population of parents experiencing homelessness must navigate is the pressure to hide their homeless circumstances from employers. As rents have skyrocketed in recent years, more employed people (and more employed parents) have lacked adequate housing and found themselves homeless (Battarai, 2024). One in four workers spend more than 50% of their income on housing. These workers are embarrassed about their circumstances, feel they have failed, and worry about social services or their employers finding out about their (and their children's) homelessness. In addition, they may be concerned that their residential status may directly or indirectly impact their ability to remain employed, which would further complicate their ability to achieve financial and residential stability.

CONNECTION TO FAMILY

The previous sections illustrated how youth can experience homelessness in a variety of different ways. As we mentioned before, a young person's relationship to their family can determine whether they face housing instability alone or with the support of their parents, guardians, or other relatives. The presence or lack of a parent/guardian can change what options exist for housing support as well as the size of the social network. In the absence of a guardian, a young person may have to take on the responsibility of finding housing, which is not generally a concern of individuals until they become adults.

Three primary reasons have emerged for why young people end up unaccompanied. First, a young person may be fleeing an unhealthy or unsafe family environment, to avoid an abusive situation or because of family conflict. Second, and related, a young person may be running from a foster care placement. While some youth in foster care are unable to conform to living in a structured environment, others experience unhealthy or abusive residential situations in the foster care system. Finally, a young person may be pushed out by family. The parent or guardian may not have the financial means to support the youth or may have personal issues that result in pushing the child out of the home. Some youth are forced to leave the family home because the parents do not agree with the young person's sexual orientation, gender identity, or other issues.

Relationship to Family

Accompanied: Individuals who are under 18 and live with a parent or guardian in an unstable environment.

Unaccompanied: Adolescents living without a parent or guardian in an unstable or inadequate space (e.g., on the street or in an abandoned building).

Forced with out: A young person who was asked to leave home by a parent or other adult in the household and prevented from returning home.

Systems: Young people who have been involved in government systems, such as juvenile justice and foster care, due to abuse, neglect, incarceration, or family homelessness.

RURAL, SUBURBAN, AND URBAN CONTEXTS

The geographic context of residential instability influences how the families and students experience homelessness and mobility. Rural, suburban, and urban school districts are all experiencing increased percentages of students experiencing homelessness, residential mobility, and housing instability. Urban areas tend to have more social service resources and shelters than either suburban or rural areas. That does not mean that services are in one building or even within walking distance of one another. An individual may have to travel several miles by bus or train to deal with different support programs, such as shelters, long-term housing support, food stamps, job training, counseling, medical services, and others. The transportation difficulties coupled with long wait times often means that an individual cannot take advantage of more than one service on any given day. The constant focus on surviving through the day limits the ability to take steps that may lead to long-term stability. In cities, some aspects of homelessness may be visible and demand attention. Community members may encounter individuals asking for money or food on the street, drive past the lines of people waiting for a shelter to open for the night, or see campers or cars where people live. Homelessness in urban areas often has some level of visibility, and advocacy organizations often exist that push for humane treatment. Conversely, the presence of large numbers of individuals in public spaces (e.g., group encampments and individuals sleeping in trains, buses, or parks) may draw antagonistic attention that leads to demands for authorities to address or even criminalize homelessness.

Suburban homelessness tends to be less visible than urban. Except for an occasional domestic violence housing unit, most suburban areas do not have homeless shelters unless gentrification of the downtown area has pushed services out of the urban center. There may be low-budget hotels and motels where families live. Middle-income suburban communities tend to discourage the existence of social welfare housing. The perception of homeless individuals as having substance abuse and mental health challenges increases concerns about the potential harm if these individuals are in the community. In addition, the existence of homeless shelters negatively impacts property values. Many of the individuals without residential stability in suburban areas either are living doubled-up or are young people couch surfing who are disconnected from social service support.

Rural homelessness can be difficult to observe. For example, a family may be living in a tent in a wooded area or a car parked in a hidden place away from town. Many people live in campers or RVs that are parked in a relative's (or non-relative's) yard or on undeveloped land. People may live in natural features, such as caves. Rural areas often offer an abundance of structures not intended to house people—abandoned barns, old livestock shelters, and disused equipment sheds. Such marginal housing makes rural people experiencing homelessness particularly vulnerable in poor or extreme weather. The lack of population concentration may make it difficult for the community to see the issue. Young people who are couch surfing may find it even more difficult to secure transportation between different locations given the lack of public transportation in rural communities. Resources and services tend to be scarcer and more difficult to access in rural areas. Families may have to travel great distances to get access to services, but they may not have transportation to do so.

HOMELESSNESS DUE TO COMMUNITY-LEVEL CATASTROPHE

Up to this point, we discussed what homelessness looks like and how it manifests at school using the model of individual and family circumstances. Increasingly, though, entire communities and entire school communities find themselves facing all the complexities of homelessness seemingly overnight, when they never expected to have these issues or to be required to participate in finding the solutions. What is being discussed here is climate-caused disaster and conflict-caused refugee situations.

To illustrate one situation, Lahaina, Maui, Hawai'i, was destroyed in a wildfire during the night of August 8, 2023, leaving 8,000 residents in search of temporary housing (Fabino, 2024). In addition, virtually all the public schools were destroyed or unusable due to toxic ash. This resulted in 3,000 displaced students. Though this community on an idyllic Pacific island never expected to be dealing with homelessness of this magnitude, its schools, families, and children suddenly were. And still are.

As natural disasters become more frequent in many areas of the country (withestern North Carolina and Los Angeles are more recent examples), schools and communities find themselves facing large numbers of suddenly homeless students and families when, before the fire, earthquake, flood, tornado, hurricane, train derailment, or busloads of refugees, they might never have thought about students experiencing homelessness within their community at all.

Global and national economic events also impact families—especially those who were living paycheck to paycheck. The COVID-19 pandemic (2020–2022) and Great Recession (2008–2010) are two recent periods when large numbers of families lost residential stability due to national economic issues. Schools and districts need to develop plans to address the current context but also be flexible to adjust strategy if (and when) an issue hits the local community, state, or nation that leads to students losing economic and residential security.

IMPACT OF CONTEXT ON SCHOOLING

Mobility and residential instability create significant challenges for students. Chapter 3 illustrates the diversity of residential instability and how these different arrangements impact young people. Here we provide a more general summary of how homelessness influences educational participation and outcomes.

Consistently moving residences influences students' ability to access school. Each resident shift requires a decision to be made about finding transportation to school, registering at a new school, or forgoing school. While educators may perceive dealing with school as a top priority, families and youth may be more focused on meeting basic needs. In addition, navigating the bureaucracy of locating transportation and negotiating school registration are huge challenges. The stress and psychological impacts of these issues are explored further in Chapter 7.

The lack of stable residence can have some unexpected consequences. Students may have a difficult time washing clothes to wear to school. Space to complete homework may be limited. The students may not have consistent access to resources needed to fully participate in schooling, such as internet service, libraries, and extracurricular sites (i.e., internship placements, tutoring, music lessons, or animal barns). The challenges of transportation to school may result in high rates of tardiness and absenteeism. Depending upon the residential situation, these young people may also be exposed to violence, trauma, and substance abuse. All these challenges have significant impacts on participation in the educational process. Dramatic impacts on academic achievement can create holes in learning that have impacts on later academic achievement.

For many students who are homeless and highly mobile, education is one of the most stable aspects of their lives. Their residential location as well as those who reside within their residence may shift frequently and unexpectedly.

These young people may have a difficult time maintaining relationships outside of the school context. We have worked with students who speak about the importance of seeing the same teachers and students when they come to school. Even though traveling a great distance to remain at the same school site may be difficult, maintaining these relationships can have important psychological impacts for the student. The mandate of McKinney-Vento to require schools to allow students to remain at their school of attendance and for the district to provide transportation is rooted in research that supports the importance of maintaining social networks. In addition, remaining in the same school allows students to have access to a consistent course curriculum.

CHAPTER CONCLUSION

Homelessness encompasses multiple different forms of residential experiences and reflects the complex array of social issues connected with poverty. Students bring these challenges with them to school, which impacts all aspects of the educational process. Understanding this reality is an important aspect of creating supportive educational spaces. Carefully exploring how students experience homelessness in the local context can help educators begin conceptualizing how to create systems with the potential to increase the likelihood of educational access and success.

Guiding Questions for Individual and/or Group Reflection

1. What aspects of the context discussed in this chapter relate to your school, district, and/or state? How does this influence how you approach working with students and families?
2. Have you had challenges supporting students who are highly mobile? What has been most difficult? Are there solutions that have worked well?
3. How does the geographic context of your school and district frame how students experience mobility? What support systems would help students overcome these challenges? How could you be part of advocating for or implementing these solutions?

Professional Learning Community Activities

Activity 1: Exploring the Local Context of Education

What is the context or contexts of homelessness and housing insecurity within your school, district, or state? Even at the school site level, multiple contexts may exist. For example, a homeless shelter or motel where people live may be in one area while doubled-up families live in another area served by the school. After identifying the different contexts, discuss the following:

- What do each of the general contexts look like? Are students connected with family? Are the areas rural, urban, or suburban?
- How does each context shape how students and families engage with the educational system? What are the educational needs of students in each context?
- What are the resources available in each context? What are the challenges that may exist in each context?
- How do your school, district, or state educators connect with students and families in each context? Are there policies and practices that create challenges for these students?

After all the information has been gathered, develop a plan of action for how to effectively integrate what has been learned into current policies and practices—consider the ecology of promise framework as you develop the plan. There may be other educators within and outside of the school or district that need to be involved in these discussions and planning.

Activity 2: Responding to Unplanned Mobility

As aforementioned, unplanned mobility negatively impacts students' educational experiences. Gather some information to inform decision-making:

- How often does unplanned mobility occur within your school, district or state?
- How does students' unplanned mobility impact educators who work with them?
- Are there predictable patterns or trends related to unplanned mobility?
- Are there things that could be done to support these students and their families when they experience unplanned mobility? Do they have access to information about resources? Are there policies that could facilitate continuation at the school even during mobility? How could community groups assist in supporting students and families?

Activity 3: Responding to a Community- or State-Level Crisis

Students often are impacted when a community- or state-level crisis occurs, including a forest fire, flood, tornado, hurricane, or other disaster that impacts housing. Educators can explore how to react to a situation as well as proactive strategies to prepare for future issues.

- Past crisis—Has your community or state experienced a crisis in the past? If so, how did the school, district, and state respond? What aspects were successful? What could be improved in the future?
- Current situation—Are there students and families who continue to be impacted by previous crises? (For example, a hurricane occurred 2 years ago but some families remain displaced.) If so, what support do these students need to fully engage in school?
- Future planning—How do the school, district, and state plan for future crises that may occur? Could an existing plan be revised to prepare for potential residential displacement of students? If there is not a plan, what could be the process of developing one?

Activity 4: Visualizing Student Experiences

A team of educators created a research-informed tool that illustrates the realities that students experiencing homelessness navigate while pursuing their education. They developed a free digital comic book entitled *Uprooted: Voices of Student Homelessness* (https://smu-uprooted.squarespace.com/). After reading the short comic book, discuss whether and how the stories that were featured reflect the experiences of students and families in your school, district, or state. Are there challenges that you had not thought about previously?

CHAPTER 7

Impact of Homelessness on Education

Educators have long understood the importance of family and community characteristics in relation to educational outcomes. Family and neighborhood demographics play a role in how students navigate and engage in the educational process. Students from low-income families and communities often face significant challenges that negatively impact their pursuit of a high school diploma. Scholars and educators alike have begun exploring how young people experience these challenges differently to create interventions that meet the students where they are; this is particularly important for students experiencing homelessness.

While some schools and districts recognize that they have a significant population of students experiencing homelessness, many other educational institutions are unaware of the size or even the existence of this subpopulation among their students. A common perception of homelessness recognizes only the most visible forms. The situation of students who lack residential stability tends to be invisible to the schools and districts they attend because they are not on the streets like the stereotyped homeless population.

Homelessness and housing insecurity among youth and their families remains at high levels. Almost all educational institutions enroll students who meet the federal definition of homelessness, and many have substantial numbers of them. For the school year 2021–2022 (the most recent data available), official reports put the number of students experiencing homelessness at 1.2 million, or 2.4% of the entire U.S. school population. Recent studies suggest, however, that this official count may drastically underreport the actual number of students facing homelessness (Cutuli et al., 2024). The researchers in this study used nine strategies (in addition to typical district procedures) to identify students experiencing homelessness within the district. Some of these strategies included looking at the home address that families listed to cross-check against local homeless and domestic violence shelter addresses, examining records for more than one family unit listing the same home address, and identifying student addresses that had been deemed as substandard or boarded-up properties according to official property records (Cuturi et al., 2024). Those last two categories, substandard or boarded-up property, could have had a student such as Brandon (see his story below) living in them and still trying to attend school in almost impossible circumstances.

Brandon Learns to Hate School

Brandon, a shy 8-year-old, lived with his mother in an abandoned building while he was repeating 2nd grade. Attending school was a challenge. They often had to move locations with minimal advance notice when a police officer or building owner found them and told them to leave. Brandon and his mom would then wander around the city until they found another temporary location. They had run out of family and friends who were willing to let them stay in their home. The constant movement made getting to school difficult. At times, they would end up in a new part of the city where his mom did not really know the transportation system. In addition, she did not have access to an alarm to make sure they were up in time to get Brandon to school. After a while, his mom got tired of being scolded by the school office staff when she would bring Brandon to school late. So he only came to school on the days that his mom could get him to class on time, which was about once a week. Brandon's love for school slowly diminished as kids made fun of him for falling behind in school and not having clean clothes. While he enjoyed learning, he already had decided that he "hated school."

As Brandon's story shows, most children experiencing homelessness live within a family unit. This is one of the fastest-growing subpopulations of homeless children and youth. A United States Department of Housing and Urban Development (HUD) report demonstrates that most youth in homeless situations under the age of 18 live within a family unit (Henry et al., 2013). Approximately 96% of youth experiencing homelessness under the age of 18 live as part of a family as compared to 34% of those between 18 and 24 years old. The homeless population also includes a significant number of teenage parents who negotiate survival along with their educational pursuits as well as those of their children (Perlman et al., 2014). In addition, students of color tend to be disproportionately impacted by residential instability. African Americans in urban areas and Native Americans in rural areas tend to disproportionately experience homelessness (Henry et al., 2021).

Lacking a stable residence significantly impacts young people. This likely does not come as a surprise. Much of what is known about education and child development suggests that stability is a prerequisite to healthy human development. Research demonstrates that homelessness significantly impacts students even when compared to other students living in poverty. For example, Brumley and colleagues (2015) controlled for other co-occurring attributes (e.g., race, class, gender) in their analysis and found that homelessness increased the likelihood of academic disengagement. Even students living doubled-up (which may look more like stable housing from the outside than a shelter, hotel, or parked van) have lower academic outcomes than their low-income peers with stable housing (Low et al., 2017). Students experiencing homelessness endure experiences that differ from their low-income peers'. To succeed academically, most students experiencing homelessness will need support that addresses their unique needs.

In this chapter, we provide an overview of the research related to homelessness and educational engagement. We draw from the challenges presented to set a foundation for the potential interventions, policies, and programming discussed in the remainder of the book.

In the sections that follow, we outline the multifaceted educational challenges that youth in homeless situations endure. We begin with a discussion of the difference between planned and unplanned residential mobility. We report that students experiencing residential instability place significant value on education but tend to perform at low levels. Then we address the trauma that frames the students' experiences. We also explain the connection between homelessness and special education. We include a section exploring the role some teachers have taken on to help meet the needs of students experiencing homelessness.

The final section emphasizes that recovery is possible. With the appropriate adjustments in policy and practice, students experiencing homelessness can succeed in school and life. We recognize that engaging with the challenges can feel overwhelming. Naming the problem is an important foundation for creating an action plan. However, dedicating time and energy to this issue may feel futile if the assumption is that nothing can be done to improve the situation. Throughout this book, we include practical ways to support students and families.

EDUCATION AS A PATH TO STABILITY

For almost two decades, we have studied the educational experiences of youth without residential stability. Consistently, these youth express how important school is to them (see Carolina's story). Most youth we have encountered aspire to complete a high school diploma and earn a college degree or postsecondary credential at a trade school. In addition to believing that education has the potential to increase the likelihood of future stability, many of the youth we have worked with identify school as the most stable aspect of their lives. While many other things may change, school has the potential to remain consistent if they can find a ride to get there. This is one of the reasons that advocates have fought to allow students to remain at their school of origin throughout their homeless experience and to have the district cover the costs of transportation (see Chapter 5).

Carolina Sees School as a Way Out

As Carolina, a 14-year-old living in a family shelter, noted, "School is very important to me." She planned to attend the local university—the same university her mother had aspired to attend, but could not afford. Carolina explained, "My mom does everything she can to make sure I'm prepared for school, even though we're homeless and in a shelter right now; she makes sure I did my homework and that I have a way to school." She hoped to earn a college scholarship as a way to "pay back" her mom.

The youth and their families clearly understand the challenges of enduring residential transience and being unable to participate in gainful employment. They connect educational achievement with future stability. However, many barriers exist that challenge their ability to fully engage in the educational process. By the time individuals experiencing homelessness reach young adulthood (18 to 24 years old), they tend to be disengaged from the educational process. Many feel they are too far behind at this point in life to complete a high school diploma, and the culmination of their negative educational experiences leads them to believe education no longer has a role in their lives. Most of the advocates for individuals experiencing homelessness we have spoken with emphasize the importance of increasing access to PK–12 education because it is far more difficult to reengage young adults who have come to believe that they do not fit within the educational system.

Not all youth experiencing homelessness can attend school regularly. Naomi Nichols (2014) documented the lives of unaccompanied homeless teenagers who resided in a shelter. She found that navigating the complex social service systems along with the many challenges associated with survival requires a significant amount of time and mental energy. The social welfare programs (e.g., food stamps, caseworkers, and housing support) generally are not coordinated. In many cities, the young person needs to travel to various parts of town to get access to the different support services. In addition, the individual may engage in off-the-books sorts of activities to survive. Nichols suggests that this "youth work" often distracts students experiencing homelessness from fully accessing the educational system, especially those who become detached from parents or a legal guardian. Even though young people consistently identify the importance of education for their future stability, at times they feel the need to prioritize meeting basic needs to survive. The 2022 Pulitzer Prize–winning novel *Demon Copperhead* by Barbara Kingsolver, set in Appalachia, paints a moving (though fictionalized) portrait of how such youth work exists side-by-side with traditionally visible forms of social support.

While we focus on traditional PK–12 institutions, we want to call out the importance of continuing education opportunities for young people who may have disengaged from school and attempt to return later. Most school districts have programs to enable youth up to about the age of 21 to complete a high school diploma. While these programs generally exist outside of the traditional school setting, we encourage these educators to consider how homelessness and housing insecurity may be influencing their students. The recommendations within this book could be adapted to improve the educational access and outcomes of students in these programs.

IMPACT ON ACADEMIC OUTCOMES

Homelessness influences education outcomes. Even when compared to students living in poverty, the experience of homelessness negatively affects students' performance in school. Residential instability dramatically impacts students' ability to fully access and participate in preschool through high school programming. Only about 68% of students experiencing homelessness graduation from high school, which is 12% lower than low-income peers who are stably housed and 18% lower than the overall student population (SchoolHouse Connection, 2025.) However, in some states, the graduation rate is 50% or lower (Freeman & Hamilton, 2008; NCHE, 2022). Youth homelessness is also a significant predictor of homelessness and housing insecurity in adulthood (Morton & Horwitz, 2019).

Lasting Impacts

The educational impacts of homelessness continue even after a student is stably housed. Students who experienced any episode of homelessness within the last three years score at the same lower proficiency rates as currently homeless students. Formerly homeless students score well below low-income peers with no history of housing instability; poverty alone cannot explain the impact of homelessness on student achievement. Recognizing homeless and formerly homeless students as a unique cohort may be the first step in designing solutions that meet their support needs and help them overcome educational deficits.

—Institute for Children, Poverty and Homelessness (2016)

According to the National Center for Homeless Education (NCHE, 2021), youth experiencing homelessness had low proficiency rates in reading (language arts) (29%), math (24%), and science (26%) for the school year 2018–2019. These estimates include test scores for only approximately a third of registered students experiencing homelessness—those who were in school the days the exams were taken—and, of course, do not account for the homeless students not registered for school. These findings likely overestimate the academic proficiency of students experiencing homelessness. Those students who miss school more frequently as well as those not registered for school presumably would have even lower scores on academic proficiency exams. A study of New York state public schools reveals a significantly lower rate of achievement for youth in homeless situations—only 19% for math and 20% for English (New York Equity Coalition, 2017). Youth in stable housing who had experienced homelessness during their school years had identical low proficiency rates—19% for math and 20% for English. As a group, students who were homeless or formerly homeless scored significantly below their peers who had never experienced homelessness. The peers achieved 42% proficiency in math and 40% proficiency in English. One important finding from this study in New York is that the educational challenges associated with a homeless experience persisted even after years of a stable residence. Schools and districts might consider how to continue supporting the students even after they obtain housing because the trauma of homelessness may have lasting impacts.

It is important to reemphasize that homelessness affects the academic performance of students who experience it in a particularly negative way, one that leads to lower test scores in every subject than even typical low-income students and students who were ever English language learners, groups that also, historically, have struggled. The only high-need group that performed lower than students experiencing homelessness in a California study were foster youth (Guinan & Lafortune, 2024), which is another subgroup of students that have experienced trauma and often high mobility rates. This study also found that students experiencing homelessness lost more ground in math and English during the pandemic and gained the least back post-pandemic, compared to other high-need student groups. Clearly, these students could use educational support. Our goal is not to suggest that one subgroup of students is more deserving than another, but rather to explain how homelessness and housing insecurity influence education in order to explore potential supports to improve educational outcomes.

Cutuli and colleagues (2013) argue that math achievement may be particularly influenced by homelessness. They found that math instruction involves learning several different operations; for example, algebra and geometry may be related but need to be learned separately. Attending school inconsistently can lead to significant gaps in mathematical knowledge and understanding. While English and language arts learning are also affected, reading tends to be a cumulative learning process and students can acquire basic skills incrementally through practice. As in the New York City study, they found no evidence that students "catch up" in English, language arts, or math after being rehoused. The students would need targeted interventions to help them academically recover.

Obradovic and colleagues (2009) also found that homelessness and high rates of mobility impact reading and math in a significant way. Without significant intervention, the impacts will persist as the student navigates the educational system. They argue that early experiences of homelessness have a "cascading" impact—a homeless episode in elementary school creates educational deficits that magnify as the student progresses through middle and high school. The Institute for Children, Poverty and Homelessness's 2016 report shows that homelessness has a greater impact on performance as students get older. Students have a more difficult time catching up in middle and high school because the more complex content gets delivered more quickly. This partially explains why educational impacts may persist beyond the point when the student secures stable housing—the gaps in learning that emerged during the time of instability would need to be addressed to ensure that the student could fully access a more advanced curriculum.

Being homeless correlates with missing school. A study conducted in Seattle found that over 60% of students experiencing homelessness in 9th grade had missed at least 6 days of school and failed at least one class—as compared to only 38% of low-income and 48% of special education students (Road Map Project, 2015). This study confirms previous research that demonstrates the increased likelihood of suspension/expulsion and decreased likelihood of accessing rigorous classes. Ingram and colleagues (2016) found that 60% of students who had experienced homelessness in their study felt that residential instability impacted their ability to stay enrolled in school. Over 40% of their participants had dropped out of school at least once. They also interviewed homeless liaisons: two-thirds felt that districts needed to do a better job of re-enrolling students who dropped out because of homelessness.

Some young people live for extended periods of time without residential stability. We have interviewed teenagers who are third-generation homeless. Even for those families that achieve stability, homelessness impacts young people well beyond the actual episode of residential instability. Policy, practice, and research tend to focus on the actual incident of homelessness with the assumption that negative impacts disappear once the student gets a stable residence. The Institute for Children, Poverty and Homelessness (2016) urges schools and districts to recognize students who are homeless or formerly homeless as a unique cohort of students. Doing so would enable programming and interventions to be developed at the school or classroom level that may encourage academic progress and achievement. This likely would involve an assessment of the gaps that exist and then supplemental instruction to enable the student to learn the content missed during residential transitions. Providing this support could be done in partnership with community groups that provide tutoring or other forms of educational interventions.

TRAUMA AND PSYCHOLOGICAL DEVELOPMENT

Lacking a stable residence is associated with many high-risk and traumatic situations. Brumley and colleagues (2015) found that adverse experiences parents and guardians endure negatively influence their children. A mother, for example, who experiences physical or sexual abuse may have psychological issues that frame her ability to be fully present for her children. For parents and guardians in homeless situations, they may also have to dedicate a concerted amount of their time and energy to meeting basic needs as well as to dealing with their own traumas associated with residential instability. That is not to say that these individuals are inadequate parents or that their children should be taken from them, which could result in more trauma for both the child and adult. However, they may need additional support to limit the impact of homelessness on their ability to care for the child.

Families in homelessness situations often get separated and experience conflict. The pressures of instability coupled with the crises that led to losing a stable home can be difficult for families to negotiate. In addition, places of refuge tend to force individuals to live in crowded spaces, which fuels additional conflict. For example, families living in a doubled-up residence may have all the immediate family members living within one room of an apartment. This could mean a mother and two or more children. We worked with a senior in high school who slept in the closet so he could have privacy; his mother and two younger siblings shared the small bedroom, another family unit used the living room, while a third family unit occupied the remaining bedroom in the small apartment. Especially as children enter middle and high school, the confined spaces create significant pressure.

The parents and guardians may lose vital support networks that could assist with finding housing and caring for the children. As aforementioned, most individuals begin their experiences with residential instability by seeking refuge in the home of a friend or family member. These doubled-up experiences typically end when a conflict occurs, which may result in a severed relationship. In addition, individuals often must move to new communities to take advantage of shelters or if another housing arrangement presents itself. This constant movement can fragment both the child's and the family's networks. As Portwood and colleagues (2015) argue, "The lives of homeless children, like those of their mothers, are frequently characterized by residential instability, separation, violence, emotional and behavioral problems, physical ailments, and constrained developmental and educational achievement" (p. 2). In the process of movement, the children may also get separated from their parents and guardians. Navigating life without familial support can create many challenges, including an increased likelihood of being exposed to different forms of abuse and exploitation.

Multifaceted Trauma

Ingram and colleagues (2016) found that 82% of participants in their study reported that homelessness significantly impacted their overall life, including:

- Ability to feel safe (72%)
- Mental/emotional health (71%)
- Physical health (62%)
- Self-confidence (69%)
- Relationship to family (68%)
- Relationship to friends (57%)

Nearly two-thirds of the participants stated that the shame associated with homelessness made them avoid telling teachers and staff about their residential situation.

The experiences of homelessness create multifaceted trauma. Losing a sense of stability can be associated with an overall sense of uncertainty and potential danger. The lack of residential stability tends to correlate with food insecurity and limited access to health care. These young people are at increased risk of being exposed to dangerous situations but have limited access to resources to help them deal with the resulting trauma. As a result, students experiencing homelessness have lower self-confidence as well as increased rates of mental and physical health issues. Canfield and colleagues (2015) suggest that homelessness exacerbates many of the challenges that exist in low-income communities. While they caution against assuming that all students without residential stability have the same challenges, they do encourage educators to carefully review academic outcomes to identify those who appear to need significant intervention.

Jasmine Attempts to Survive Homelessness

Jasmine, a 17-year-old with sophomore-level credits, lived in an emergency youth shelter. She had lived on her own for over a year, since being kicked out of her family home after an argument with her father about an older boyfriend. She had to support herself financially even before she could work legally; meeting basic needs was difficult. After couch surfing among friends for about a year, she ended up without a place to stay. She found herself living in an abandoned building near the downtown area and met an older man who got her involved in prostitution to meet basic needs, which also led to drug addiction. Soon after turning 17, she sought refuge in the youth shelter and began working toward a GED and receiving counseling. She was proud of her progress, but worried about what would happen when she turned 18 and had to leave the shelter. To complicate matters, she had become pregnant shortly before escaping prostitution. The shelter staff and her social worker were trying to find space in one of the shelters that served pregnant mothers so Jasmine could continue school and therapy—and hopefully become stabilized as she transitioned to adulthood.

Young people experiencing homelessness are more likely to engage in substance use and abuse than their housed peers. They are also more likely to endure physical and sexual abuse. Unaccompanied teenagers may resort to "survival sex" or other forms of exploitation in order to meet basic needs. As Jasmine's story illustrates, the exposure to these multiple risk factors negatively impacts the ability to fully take advantage of school unless given additional support. As will be discussed in later chapters, these additional supports frequently require collaboration between the school and community organizations. These young people need comprehensive and coordinated support to negotiate the multiple risk factors associated with homelessness.

Youth in homeless situations endure multiple forms of trauma that frame how they view life and engage with the educational system. The American Institutes for Research released a 2014 "report card" on childhood homelessness. This report confirmed how lacking stability and being exposed to the previously discussed risk factors associated with homelessness during childhood can have a dramatic impact on children's cognitive and social development. In a review of current research, the authors argue that "early traumatic experiences can have profound effects on the brain architecture of young children that lead to altered brain size and structure leading to impaired cognitive skills, memory, emotional self-regulation, behavioral problems, coping and social relationships" (Bassuk et al., 2014, p. 82).

Homelessness also correlates with an increased likelihood of suicidal ideation. The social shame, sense of helplessness, and exposure to other forms of trauma can have a significantly negative impact on the young person's perception of the world. Without adequate counseling and support, they may consider ending their lives to escape. Unfortunately, we have known young people who lost their lives in this way. The persistent instability and trauma can seem inescapable, especially if they do not have a caring adult who can provide guidance and encouragement.

Some advocates for youth experiencing homelessness have begun using Post-Traumatic Stress Disorder (PTSD) to name the challenges. However, the "post" aspect of the diagnosis does not work well for individuals who remain in the situation that is causing the trauma. For students who do regain housing stability, the label of PTSD helps capture the enduring nature of residential instability (and related traumas). To address the importance of the continued exposure of individuals without residential stability, "persistent" or "perpetual" would be better identifiers for traumatic stress. Other advocates have used the term "chronic PTSD" to capture the ongoing experiences of trauma. Instead of working therapeutically only on issues related to the past, these young people also need guidance with continued stress and trauma. They need tools to deal with their current situation and to develop hope for a future of stability.

Residential instability is more than just lacking housing. The young people and their families endure the multiple traumas associated with instability. Research consistently demonstrates that these families want their children to have educational opportunities and that the students value education. However, they need assistance negotiating the barriers and dealing with the trauma.

SPECIAL EDUCATION AND COGNITIVE DEVELOPMENT

In reviewing research, Ingram and colleagues (2016) found that youth experiencing homelessness are four times more likely to have developmental delays and more than twice as likely to have a learning disability (Institute for Children, Poverty & Homelessness, 2024). The negative influence of a homeless episode occurs quickly and then grows over time. Ingram and colleagues argue,

> Studies show that once a child or youth becomes homeless, they enter into negative developmental pathways that often result in chronic homelessness . . . it is therefore essential that schools work as part of the mechanism that identifies homeless youth quickly, and connects them to the services that can help stabilize their housing, keep them in their community, and get them back on track. (p. 14)

The developmental impacts on students often lead to academic challenges and potentially an assessment for special education services.

Youth experiencing homelessness qualify for special education services at a disproportionately high rate. The National Center for Homeless Education (Endres & Cidade, 2015) reports that 17% of youth in homeless situations qualify for special education services (as compared to 12% of the general student population). A study of Chicago Public Schools (Dworsky, 2008) found that these students tend to be identified as having emotional/behavior disorders or learning disabilities. The likelihood of carrying a special education label increased as the student progressed through elementary and middle school. In Dworsky's study, the percentage of students with a special education label peaked in 9th grade at 36%. She suggests the following consideration:

> The unusually high percentage of children with special education needs among families in our study raises particular concerns. Schools must make concerted effort to identify homeless children with individualized education plans when they first enroll, and monitor the implementation of those IEPs. At the same time, care must be taken to differentiate the effects of homelessness and school mobility on school performance from learning and other disabilities (n.p.).

As aforementioned, the increased likelihood of a student in a homeless situation being labeled as having emotional or learning challenges may not be surprising. These young people experience significant levels of trauma and educational disruption.

Educators and school leaders should carefully consider when and how to determine if a student experiencing homelessness has a disability versus if they only need supplemental educational support negotiating the educational challenges associated with being homeless. Trying to determine if a student should be identified as having a disability can be a difficult task. Schools and districts may have few supplemental resources to address these issues. Giving the special education label could be seen as a way to allow the student to access needed resources. However, if a student is not truly in need of special education services, offering additional resources and programming that address the unique needs of students experiencing homelessness would be more appropriate than placing the student in special education. Trevon's story below illustrates the complexity of distinguishing between a mental health issue and a rational emotional response to trauma. Clearly, Trevon required additional psychological support as well as tools to deal with the social challenges associated with being homeless.

Trevon's Story

Trevon, a 17-year-old Black male, was in a 10th-grade Special Day Class. His father died of a heart attack when Trevon was 11 years old. For the past several years, Trevon had alternated between living with his mother and at a youth shelter. When he could not find a place to stay, he would ride the city train from "station to station" for up to 3 days in a row without eating. Trevon explained, "I felt sad, I mean, I got upset because of what was goin' on . . . the hardest part was I couldn't even get to school during that time, you know, plus, I already be knowing I be missing my credits and I was getting close to getting kicked out anyways." He had a difficult time making friends because he kept moving to different schools and he avoided letting other students get too close because they might find out about his living situation. Shame covered his life. Trevon started to get into fights when other students made fun of him and he got sent to the principal several times. He admitted to having "behavior" problems that led to him being placed in special education. Education was important to him: "Without school you won't be able to get a job or have a place to live or anything." He worried about continuing to be homeless in the future, especially once he turned 18 in a few months and was no longer qualified to live in a youth shelter. He worried that he would die soon after turning 18 because that is what happens to kids on the street.

For the students who do qualify for special education services, consistently gaining access to services while homeless can be a challenge. Students who do not consistently attend school may miss meetings with psychologists, resource specialists, speech therapists, and other service providers. Unplanned movement between schools may not allow for an immediate transfer of the Individual Education Plan (IEP) and documentation of progress toward goals. Preserving consistent access to special education and other supplemental services is another reason why educational advocates encourage school sites and districts to ensure that students have access to transportation to enable them to remain at the school site of origin throughout their homeless experiences.

RECOVERY IS POSSIBLE

The issues addressed in this chapter can seem overwhelming. As educators gain a deeper understanding of the challenges associated with youth homelessness, it is easy to assume that solutions would be nearly impossible to identify and implement. Obviously, our goal in sharing this information is not to discourage individuals. However, knowing the significant challenges these young people and their families face is the first step to begin conceptualizing how to develop a local response. Further, there are clear guidelines and support via McKinney-Vento policy. This book aims to support educators in their understanding, implementation, and evaluation of McKinney-Vento with student success and well-being as a critical barometer of its effectiveness.

Not all youth have the same experience with homelessness. We present a range of issues in this chapter that are associated with youth homelessness and how they influence educational participation; however, each young person's experience differs. Some students will need a significant amount of support to access school, while others would benefit from a few seemingly minor policy changes or access to counseling. Simply having a school staff who view students experiencing homelessness as *students* and homelessness as merely a situation they are experiencing—not a permanent aspect of their identity—can go a long way toward creating a supportive environment. For example, students who were gifted before their family lost their home due to unemployment are still gifted even though they are now living doubled-up with relatives. A youth who is a dedicated athlete who finds himself couch surfing due to intense conflict with a parent is still a youth for whom athletics is important.

In the final section of this book, we provide strategies and recommendations to support students in ways that recognize their multidimensional personalities, experiences and goals.

CHAPTER CONCLUSION

Homelessness clearly influences the educational process. The impacts of residential instability outlast the episode of homelessness. Students and families recognize the positive short- and long-term aspects of school, but the daily struggles of survival can limit full engagement in the educational process. The students who succeed are often those who get connected to services and integrated support. The final section of the book will explore this concept further.

Guiding Questions for Individual and/or Group Reflection

1. How are the students identified as homeless performing academically in your school or district? How does their performance compare to other students'?
2. What other services do these students qualify for (e.g., special education, gifted and talented, counseling)? What challenges and successes do students experience in fully accessing these services?
3. What forms of trauma do students without residential stability who attend your school or district experience? How do you see these influencing the educational process?

Professional Learning Community Activities

Activity 1: Engaging With Data

Explore current school, district, or state data. How many students experiencing homelessness:

- Have special education services?
- Are English language learners?

- Are in gifted and talented education (GATE) programs?
- Are taking advanced placement or dual enrollment?
- Receive counseling support from the school?
- Participate in other supplemental supports?

After gathering data, consider the following:

- Does their participation in programs differ from their peers'?
- How effective have these programs been? Do the outcomes differ for students experiencing homelessness as compared to their peers?
- How do the educators who work with the students in the classroom and across the supplement programs collaborate to support the students?
- Consider the ecology of promise approach. Are there opportunities to adjust programming to improve support?

Activity 2: Reflecting on Previous Student Successes

Consider students who experienced homelessness and achieved academic success, which can differ depending upon the age group of the students in the school (and district-or state-level educators can look at longer trajectories than school-site educators). What helped the students succeed? Avoid giving too much attention to aspects of the student that are difficult to change, such as personality. Did the students utilize certain educational supports? Were there classes or classroom activities that motivated that student? What community supports were the students using? After considering why and how the students were able to achieve success, explore ways to leverage this knowledge to expand these supports for other students.

Part III

MOVING BEYOND ACCESS

CHAPTER 8

Adjusting and Aligning School and District Policies

School sites and districts play important roles in supporting students without residential stability. The structure of school reform efforts can create both opportunities and challenges. While acknowledging the challenges associated with policy incoherence, we spend the majority of this chapter discussing how to integrate these students within educational access and success efforts already embedded within most public educational institutions.

POLICY INCOHERENCE AND CHURN

Adding students' homelessness, high mobility, and residential instability to schools' and districts' plates (or escalating these issues' visibility and urgency if they already are on the plate) is no small undertaking. In addition to the complexity of these issues themselves and their connections to larger societal injustices and inequities, such as racism, classism, inadequate mental health care, domestic violence, and so forth (Aviles de Bradley, 2015; McKenzie-Mohr et al., 2011), policy formulation, implementation, and evaluation around any issue in U.S. schools and districts have long histories characterized by incoherence, randomness, politicization, and what Hess (1998) described as "policy churn." He defined school policy churn as "an endless stream of new initiatives, with the schools and teachers never having time to become comfortable with any given change" (p. 52). Teachers and administrators may adjust their practices to align with a given policy only to have a new mandate from the district, county, or state that requires a different—not necessarily better—approach. After a while, educators may become frustrated by the constant changes that do not seem to be improving outcomes.

Such churn is typically not the exception in school and district policy, but rather it is the normal situation, with each new year, new leader, new school board, new legislative session, and new professional development consultant bringing a new wave of initiatives that seldom are integrated into a coherent vision, evaluated, or even formally abandoned if ineffective. Sebring and Bryk

(2000) identified a similar phenomenon at the school campus level with their description of "Christmas tree schools" that emerged from a long-term study of school reform in Chicago. This phrase referred to schools that were "well-known showcases because of the variety of programs they boasted. Frequently, however, these programs were uncoordinated . . . like dazzling ornaments hung on a tree at Christmas, but basic school operations remained unattended" (p. 3). Continuing to add programs and policies without a coherent mission that guides and integrates the efforts together rarely has a positive influence on student outcomes.

Thus, the revised McKinney-Vento Act's and ESSA's requirements that schools, districts, and states review all policies to determine how they might impact students experiencing homelessness and high mobility adds another layer to (likely) an already chaotic policy environment (NAEHCY, 2016). School and district leaders often only have a vague understanding about how local policies and practices impact any of their general or special populations of students (Hess, 1998).

Furthermore, although federal legislation articulates some specific areas where review must take place, it does little to help identify which local policies and practices might need the closest review or which might present the most challenges for integration with requirements contained within the acts themselves. In other words, much at the school and district level that prevents full participation in the educational experience for children and youth in homeless and highly mobile situations is not written down in formal policy and might instead be tied to local customs, traditional practices, or the actions and beliefs of key individuals.

Nonetheless, we can say that likely local policy candidates for review include student and family outreach efforts, enrollment and records procedures, student data systems, family assistance referral processes, counseling and mental health services, Section 504 procedures, professional development guidelines, board policies, and student handbooks. It is still up to each school and district to determine what form such a review might take, what policies would be included, how changes (if identified) would be implemented, when changes would occur, and who would be responsible for assessment and evaluation. Guidance for implementing McKinney-Vento, as amended by ESSA, was issued July 27, 2016 and amended in 2018, and is available from the U.S. Department of Education (and can also be found on the SchoolHouse Connection website).

For school and district leaders seeking guidance on reviewing, adjusting, and aligning their policies to better serve students experiencing homelessness, there is a significant body of educational research to draw from when making these important decisions. This research has documented effective responses to earlier waves of changing student demographics and to landmark legislation (e.g., Individuals with Disabilities Education Act and No Child Left Behind) that required more of schools and districts in meeting the needs of special populations of students. The next section of this chapter provides insights gleaned from this earlier body of research about state and federal policy implementation within the local context.

SCHOOL AND DISTRICT EFFECTIVENESS IN SERVING SPECIAL STUDENT POPULATIONS

Within the past several decades, a growing body of research literature has accumulated on the characteristics, cultures, and practices of schools and districts that more effectively serve students and student populations who have historically been underserved by typical models and modes of U.S. public schooling (Rorrer et al., 2008). These groups include students with learning differences, English language learners, students from low-income homes, and students from racial and ethnic backgrounds that differ from the majority in their schools, including African American and Latina/o/x students, whose achievement has typically lagged behind that of White students in the same schools. Updated reviews of the research on strategies that have proven effective for closing racial and ethnic achievement gaps at the campus level have been provided by Porter (2005), Desimone and Long (2010), and others. Calderón and colleagues (2011) reviewed effective campus-level strategies for English language learners. Additionally, district-level improvement research has become increasingly common, with studies exploring how districts more effectively serve students identified and served through special education (Samuels, 2007) and closing achievement gaps between and among student racial, ethnic, and income groups (Leithwood, 2010; Rorrer et al., 2008).

What all of this research has in common are findings that point toward the value of policy intentionality, alignment, coherence, and accountability. Like schools and districts that have experienced success with other groups historically marginalized by traditional schooling, campuses and districts that are and will be successful with students experiencing high mobility, residential instability, and homelessness must be purposeful about developing, implementing, and evaluating policies that promote such success. As researchers in the field of Total Quality Management are fond of pointing out, every system is ideally designed to produce what it is currently producing. Thus, in the absence of significant evaluation, redesign, and reform, the results of the system (i.e., school or district) will vary little from year to year. Schools and districts that are not adequately serving students who are homeless or highly mobile are very unlikely to spontaneously begin doing so. As Miller et al. (2015) phrased it, meeting the needs of students in homeless situations must be normalized within school and district operations. ESSA policy now mandates movement toward that goal.

SHIFTING AWAY FROM CHARITY APPROACHES

Miller and colleagues (2015) conducted in-depth case studies of schools and districts that responded systemically to better meet the needs of students facing homelessness. One of their findings pointed to the importance of campuses being embedded in district systems that were committed at both levels to addressing issues students and families faced as they negotiated changing housing stability. In other words, the schools and districts in Miller and colleagues' studies owned (took responsibility for) responding to these issues as part of their core work of educating students—part of the central or "normal" way of doing business in these educational settings:

> A sustained systemic response symbolizes district level commitment to the issue. It emphasizes supporting HHM [homeless and highly mobile] students as part of the district's "core work" (Spillane, 2005), thereby informing, motivating, and normalizing the engagement of homelessness beyond the central office. (p. 746)

Thus, schools and districts must make an important cultural shift to accept that students experiencing homelessness, high mobility, and residential instability are a significant portion of their regular student population and that meeting the unique needs of these students and their families is not an extraordinary part of school personnel's jobs nor the job of someone else altogether.

A district or school mission to serve all students includes those with housing instability. Achieving equitable access and success involves normalizing services for these students as part of the site and district mission. One of this book's authors (Aviles de Bradley, 2015) made this point even more forcefully in earlier work. She argued that not only are students experiencing homelessness part of the normal school situation, but that educators need to view these concerns through a lens of equity rather than one of charity and take action appropriately:

> The prevailing approach taken to address homelessness, as reflected in the erratic approach to supporting homeless students in schools, is grounded in a charitable framework. This approach is problematic due to the stigma associated with charity in which individuals (not systems) are blamed for their situations. . . . A charitable approach, while offering short-term, needed help, does little to advance significant, structural changes that support effective implementation of McKinney-Vento in schools serving students experiencing

> instability. . . . It is in the best interest of students experiencing housing instability that these methods be critically scrutinized, alternatively creating systems that do not rely on acts of charity. McKinney-Vento is not a charitable undertaking; it is a federal policy serving to ensure that the educational rights of students experiencing homelessness and their families are not violated. (pp. 18–19)

For Aviles de Bradley, then, the important policy reformulations that are needed to make homeless services part of the normal school situation require a philosophical shift away from charity and toward educational access for all students.

Other research on district approaches to meeting the needs of students in homeless circumstances has become available that also points to the importance of coherence and an equity orientation among leadership. Levin and colleagues (2023) studied "districts [that] worked hard to identify students experiencing homelessness and supplemented modest federal funds with private funding, district funding, community-based resources, and other school services to provide transportation, essential items such as food and clothing, health services, academic supports, and housing supports, wherever possible" (n.p.). These districts took broad-brush approaches, trying to effect change in many of the interlocking systems that produce the school experience that students in homeless circumstances have. Pavlakis (2018) focused specifically on how the concepts of space and place dictate what is effective policy and practice for students experiencing homelessness. Both residential place and geographic space matter intensely in solution formation. By listening and learning from the individuals and groups experiencing homelessness in a broad range of configurations, newer policy solutions and practice recommendations promote responsiveness and innovation rather than one best fit.

Thus, districts (and schools within them) must move away from blaming external factors and dismissing data that reveal ineffectiveness with historically marginalized student populations and toward accepting ownership for ensuring that *all* students have consistent access to school and the resources they need to be successful. One possibility for an approach to action on this issue is a formal (or informal) policy audit (see the "Districts as Institutional Actors in School Reform Model" summary). The next section covers what such an audit might look like.

Districts as Institutional Actors in School Reform Model

Establishing Policy Coherence

- Mediating federal, state, and local policy
- Aligning resources

Providing Instructional Leadership

- Generating will
- Building capacity

Reorienting the organization

- Refining organizational structure and process
- Changing the district culture

Maintaining and equity focus

- Owning past inequity
- Foregrounding equity

(Rorrer et al., 2008)

POLICY AUDITS

Schools and school districts are required by law to conduct, or they voluntarily engage in, a variety of audits each year. These can include fiscal audits, personnel audits, special program compliance audits, accreditation audits, curriculum audits, equity audits, and policy audits, among others (Skrla et al., 2009). Policy audits typically are solicited by districts, conducted by outside agencies (such as the state school board association), and involve reviewing federal, state, and local policies contained in district board policy manuals for currency and consistency.

A different type of policy audit could be performed by an educational institution voluntarily seeking to improve in an area where it knows there is a performance problem. A report from the National Center for Public Policy and Higher Education (Jones & Paulson, 2001) described what this type of policy audit might entail:

> Before adding new policies, programs, or procedures onto those already in place, an "audit" of the current array of policies is needed. Such an audit typically has two major components:
>
> - A systematic review of existing policies—at least those that are most obviously connected to the areas of performance that have been questioned.
> - Interviews with knowledgeable individuals who can share their understanding of what is not working and why.
>
> The objective of conducting a policy audit is to clear the underbrush—to remove barriers that would continue to be impediments even if well-designed new policies were implemented. (p. 20)

Thus, a policy audit in a school or district in the area of serving better the educational needs of students experiencing homelessness would serve the purpose of "clearing the underbrush" to allow a clear view of how local and state policies (and informal procedures, including handbooks, office routines, and school schedules) support or impede full implementation of McKinney-Vento and ESSA requirements and allow children and youth in homeless situations to fully participate in schooling in a way that is most likely to lead to their long-term educational success.

Multiple areas in a school system may need to be reviewed for effectiveness in working with students and families experiencing homelessness (see the breakout box, "Accountability from a District Leader's Viewpoint," on p. 108). As discussed in Chapter 5, areas that might be considered by such an audit as outlined by ESSA would likely include but are not limited to (U.S. Department of Education, 2016):

- Early intervention services—In coordination with the requirements found in IDEA, part C, to ensure that homeless families who have students with disabilities can access services before reaching regular school attendance age.
- Language and communication—Review if and how information is shared with students and families in ways that are accessible to them. This includes written communication on websites, registration documents, brochures, and other materials, as well as the way that educators explain resources.
- Enrollment—Newly authorized federal legislation requires that barriers to school enrollment be removed for children experiencing homelessness, including barriers created by deadlines, fines, fees, records, and absences.
- Food services—Barriers to immediate participation in school nutrition programs must be eliminated.
- Privacy rights—Schools must treat information about children and youth experiencing homelessness as a student education record, subject to all the provisions of the Family Educational Rights and Privacy Act (FERPA).
- Counseling and mental health services—Students who are homeless must have access to counseling services and referral services for mental health care.
- Extracurricular programs—School and district policies must be aligned so that students experiencing homelessness and are otherwise eligible have access to the full range of school programs, including extracurricular activities, such as athletics, cheerleading, and band.
- Transportation—The federal legislation (ESSA and McKinney-Vento) contains detailed requirements for maintaining students' enrollment

in their schools of origin and minimizing disruption to the educational settings.

- Curricular programming—Students classified as homeless, if otherwise eligible, must be able to participate in magnet school, summer school, career and technical (vocational) education, Advanced Placement, online learning, charter school programs, extended day/year, tutoring, and other enhancements and alternatives to the traditional educational program, if such are available to other students in the school/district.
- Homeless liaisons and professional development—Schools and districts that receive McKinney-Vento funding must designate homeless liaison coordinators, must ensure that these individuals have appropriate training, and the liaisons must provide training for school faculty and staff.
- Student performance tracking/accountability—ESSA now requires that state achievement report cards provide disaggregated data on graduation rates and achievement for students classified as homeless. Best practices would suggest that districts and schools collect and analyze such disaggregated data as well.

Accountability From a District Leader's Viewpoint

(From an interview with an assistant superintendent who participated in one of our research studies.)

One of the things I was really pleased with was the new process of identification [of students qualified for McKinney-Vento services] and in finding the kids and being able to provide those resources. But we still need to get better than that. It's also the attitude that they're treated to at the sites. One of the things, and this came from [the superintendent], is about customer service. Customer service and just treating those families goes a long way and it provides greater access for those families. If they're treated politely and respectfully and given a voice, then the odds of them being more successful in your system are better. We did a customer survey phone call out to all of our parents the first week of school . . . got a general idea of which sites were better than others.

It also puts the employee on notice. I don't care what that parent looks like. I don't care who those parents are. I don't care if they're living with their aunts or their uncles or their cousins or their friends or whatever, we're going to serve them like our number-one customer, period, the end. If you don't like that, resignation letters are available at the personnel office. You can go somewhere else. That's the other thing about [this district] is that we sort of are hardcore. Whatever visions we have and whatever direction we choose to go, we go. If you don't like it, we'll take care of you. You're going to perform. There's an expectation of performance here.

Because you can have the best of intentions and a lack of accountability, and nothing changes for the families because it's that front line that makes a huge difference for parents because they are not coming in to talk to me. They're going to meet [the homeless liaison] and that's nice, but they're not going to come deal with [her] on a daily basis. It's that school staff secretary, it's the yard duty, it's the cafeteria ladies or guys, it's that front line and how we open our doors to them through that. We're really working on that, too.

ACCOUNTABILITY

The literature on academic change of any sort, but that on change around homelessness particularly, is very clear—no change will begin, take root, flourish or be sustained without some sort of system that collects data on results and includes accountability for individuals and groups responsible for implementing the changes. Policy change and alignment are no different. Consider this statement from Steele and Malchiodi (2012), experts on trauma-informed practices with children and adolescents:

> No process or change is useful in the long term without accountability. All members must be committed and agree to be accountable in this process. Appropriate measures must be used frequently and consistently to help (not force) members to continually work toward aligning their practices, policies, and procedures with their values and beliefs. (p. 124)

Thus, any plan for examining and aligning school and district policies around service to children, youth, and families who are experiencing homelessness and residential instability should include a plan for assessment and accountability to ensure that changes get made and consistently integrated into school policies and practices. Do not misunderstand; we are not arguing against innovation and risk-taking. Successful districts we have studied are very clear that they do not blame people for trying things that evaluation later shows to have been ineffective. Rather, they focus on *not continuing* things that do not work and on seeking new, more effective solutions (Koschoreck, 2003).

LEADERSHIP FOR POLICY ALIGNMENT

As with almost every other aspect of schooling, success in policy adjustment and alignment around service to students and families experiencing homelessness depends on buy-in and support from school leadership. This does not necessarily have to come from people in formal positional leadership roles (see Spillane & Diamond [2006] and others' discussions of distributed leadership), but it most often is the case that, in successful examples, the formal school and district leaders have gotten on board with the changes that are needed to integrate effective education for students in residentially unstable situations into the fabric of regular school life.

A different sort of leadership is also often required. As Miller and colleagues (2013) found, "Leadership in 'social frontier' spaces is often dependent upon negotiation, entrepreneurship, and relationship brokering" (p. 543), as with our earlier example of the transportation director working with colleagues across state lines to support students qualifying for McKinney-Vento protections. In other words, making the changes in the policy arena described in this chapter will require leaders to use more "soft" relationship skills and coalition-building than they might have to use in other, more clear-cut, mandated situations and in situations in which educators feel more comfortable.

CHAPTER CONCLUSION

In this chapter, the discussion focused on what schools and districts can and should do to bring their campus and district systems into alignment to better serve the urgent and unique needs of children and youth who are homeless, highly mobile, and residentially unstable. Lessons learned from earlier research on school and district responses to federal policy initiatives have been explored, along with suggestions for policy audits and new approaches to leadership.

Guiding Questions for Individual and/or Group Reflection

1. Do you have an idea of how well-aligned your current policies and procedures at your school or district are with the requirements of McKinney-Vento, ESSA requirements, and/or your state statutes regarding the education of students experiencing homelessness?
2. If you decided to conduct a formal policy audit in this area, who would need to be involved in the process? Whose support would be essential? From which individuals and groups might you expect the most resistance?

3. How knowledgeable do you think the people in formal leadership roles in your school or district are about what policies are currently in place regarding the education of children and youth who are experiencing homelessness, high mobility, and residential instability? How informed are leaders about the requirements of McKinney-Vento, ESSA, and similar state legislation in your state?
4. How are personnel in your school and district held accountable for meeting the needs of students experiencing homelessness?

Professional Learning Community Activities

Activity 1: Letting Go of Certain Tasks

Reviewing current efforts should include a critical eye toward identifying current work that may be ineffective. At times, professional development can feel like a constant piling-on of more work and responsibility. Carefully review current practices to see whether there are tasks that could be dropped or reimagined in ways that take less time and effort; there may be duplication of effort that could be streamlined. The process can help educators create time and space to engage in new, promising practices.

Activity 2: Reviewing a Policy or Practice

Pick one area of the school and conduct a mini–policy audit. Divide the responsibility for finding relevant local and state policies, interviewing key implementation personnel, and looking at handbooks and policy documents in order to report back to the group. After gathering information, propose changes. In a high school, for example, educators could find out if a student who is experiencing homelessness can practically engage in after-school programming. In reviewing a policy or practice, consider leveraging the ecology of promise approach to identify potential challenges and solutions.

CHAPTER 9

Securing Resources and Forming Authentic, Enduring Partnerships

The mandates outlined in the McKinney-Vento Act provide guidance for implementation. We want to recognize that McKinney-Vento is an underfunded mandate, which creates challenges for districts and schools in providing robust services and programming that adequately meet the needs of students experiencing homelessness. Many schools and districts have sought out additional funding sources to address some of these funding limitations. As previously discussed, schools with higher numbers of students experiencing homelessness are often located in low-income communities that struggle with meeting other basic needs (e.g., food, housing, health care) of the students and families they serve. In this chapter, our goal is to assist educators in identifying potential funding sources and collaborations within local communities that can be leveraged to meet the educational and subsistence needs of students and their families. These collaborative partnerships will strengthen relationships between educators and community mentors, which promotes improved educational and well-being outcomes for students.

ONGOING ECONOMIC STRESS AND EDUCATIONAL CONTEXT

> We know there is far too much scarcity in this rich land. What good is all this money when so many of us take four buses to work and turn cars into homes and deal with toothaches by waiting for the rot to dull the nerves and drink water we know is poisoned? We should significantly deepen our collective investment in economic stability and basic dignity, promoting a right to a decent existence—to some minimum standard of nutrition, healthcare and other essentials of life. (Desmond, 2023, p. 122)

One factor that distinguishes the current climate for schools dealing with students in homeless circumstances is that the communities in which schools are embedded often face prolonged economic stress, disinvestment, and extraordinary demands on their social support services due to the intersection of economic and social factors that made up the U.S. recession that began in 2008. While the economy had been on a good trajectory toward "recovery," demonstrated by improvements in traditional indicators such as unemployment rates and home prices, many communities were still on shaky economic and social service footing in 2020. Vulnerable families and communities that were barely hanging on then had their footing pulled from them due to the COVID-19 pandemic. Many families were unable to recover from the loss of pay, which contributed to further housing instability and homelessness. And while the eviction moratorium allowed many families to remain in their homes, it did not prevent the accumulation of back rent and fees once the moratorium was lifted. Low-income residents who lost jobs or wages during the pandemic amassed between $11 and $53 billion in back rent, utilities, and late fees (Dougherty, 2021), leaving scores of families in many of these communities vulnerable to displacement.

The communities most impacted by these housing contexts are considered economically challenged (National Resource Network, 2015). Thus, schools seeking resources and partnerships in serving the needs of students without residential stability face greater challenges than ever before in the United States. Educators within schools and beyond play a critical role in developing collaborations that facilitate connecting students and families with resources and services that support their educational goals.

IDENTIFYING RESOURCES

McKinney-Vento and ESSA require schools and districts to cooperate with each other and with other agencies that serve the same students to work toward the goal of wraparound support. In particular, the ESSA revisions push schools, districts, and states past policies designed merely to encourage educational access and ask them to aim higher, at success and achievement. Collaborative approaches and higher goals can seem like formidable challenges for schools and districts given the fragmented nature of U.S. social and education services, the scarcity of funding, and the transitory nature of students and their families. School leaders and staff must adopt creative approaches and learn from the successes of others. Different approaches to addressing resource shortages are out there to be found and used.

Split Funding and Coordinated Services

Many of the students who qualify for services under McKinney-Vento also qualify for some services under other local, state, and federal special programs. As the U.S. Department of Education (2004) points out: "School districts, as recipients of Federal financial assistance and as public entities, must ensure that their educational programs for homeless children are administered in a nondiscriminatory manner" (p. 3). School and district services that are already organized (and possibly funded) through other programs can be used to meet educational needs for children and youth experiencing homelessness if the students also meet qualification guidelines for these other programs. For example, special education services, 504 procedures, Title I supplemental learning support, gifted and talented services, career/technology education, and so forth can be considered as avenues through which to meet an identified educational need for a student experiencing homelessness. Teacher and staff positions can also be funded from various sources to allow a variety of students with similar needs to receive support. Granted, the implementation of the services may need to be adjusted based upon the needs of students without residential stability. Educators within and outside of the school or district can discuss potential collaborations that could exist by, for example, leveraging split funding to develop an educator position that meets multiple needs and exploring how to create coordinated services that draw from multiple funding streams to meet the needs of students experiencing homelessness. These strategies tend to be more effective uses of funding than relying on siloed and uncoordinated support.

Grants

Federal and state agencies provide funding that can be used to address the educational needs of students experiencing homelessness. These grants often have specific parameters and typically involve an application process. Educators within and outside of the school or district can apply for funding—including coordinated requests that seek to provide coordinated support for students and their families. We offer a brief list of state, local, nonprofit, and private organization funding opportunities; however, we encourage educators to explore what may be available in their local and state context.

McKinney-Vento LEA Subgrants. In addition to the grant each state receives from the federal government under the McKinney-Vento Act, local educational agencies (LEAs) may be eligible to apply for subgrants to access a portion of this state funding to provide a broad range of services for students experiencing homelessness, including:

1. Tutoring, supplemental instruction, and other educational services that help homeless children and youth reach the same challenging state content and state student performance standards to which all children are held. As clearly specified in the ESEA, as reauthorized by the NCLB Act, all academic enrichment programs for disadvantaged students, including programs for homeless students, must be aligned with state

standards and curricula. Additionally, when offering supplemental instruction, LEAs should focus on providing services for children and youth that reflect scientifically based research as the foundation for programs and strategies to ensure academic success.

2. Expedited evaluations of eligible students to measure their strengths and needs. These evaluations should be done promptly to avoid a gap in the provision of necessary services to those children and youth. Evaluations may also determine a homeless child or youth's eligibility for other programs and services, including educational programs for gifted and talented students, special education and related services for children with disabilities, English language acquisition, vocational education, school lunch, and appropriate programs or services under ESEA.
3. Programs and other activities designed to raise awareness among educators and pupil services personnel of the rights of homeless children and youth under the McKinney-Vento Act, and the special needs such children and youth have because of their homelessness.
4. Referrals of eligible students to medical, dental, mental, and other health services.
5. Paying the excess cost of transportation not otherwise provided through federal, state, or local funds, to enable students to attend schools selected under section 722(g)(3) of the McKinney-Vento Act.
6. Developmentally appropriate early childhood education programs for homeless children of preschool age that are not provided through other federal, state, or local funds.
7. Services and assistance to attract, engage, and retain homeless children and youth, and unaccompanied youth, in public school programs and services provided to non-homeless children and youth.
8. Before- and after-school programs, mentoring, and summer programs for homeless children and youth. Qualified personnel may provide homework assistance, tutoring, and supervision of other educational instruction in carrying out these activities.
9. Paying fees and costs associated with tracking, obtaining, and transferring records necessary for the enrollment of students in school. The records may include birth certificates, guardianship records, immunization records, academic records, and evaluations of students needed to determine eligibility for other programs and services.
10. Education and training programs for parents of homeless children and youth regarding the rights their children have as homeless individuals and regarding the educational and other resources available to their children.

11. Programs coordinating services provided by schools and other agencies to eligible students to expand and enhance such services. Coordination with programs funded under the Runaway and Homeless Youth Act should be included in this effort.
12. Pupil services programs providing violence prevention counseling and referrals to such counseling.
13. Programs addressing the needs of eligible students that may arise from domestic violence.
14. Providing supplies to nonschool facilities serving eligible students and adapting these facilities to enable them to provide services.
15. Providing school supplies to eligible students at shelters, temporary housing facilities, and other locations as appropriate.
16. Providing extraordinary or emergency services to eligible students as necessary to enroll and retain such children and youth in school. (U.S. Department of Education, 2004, pp. 24–26)

These categories of allowable expenditures under LEA subgrants go far beyond the typical expenditures for supplies and transportation and explicitly include counseling and mental health support. Additionally, the December 2015 reauthorization of the Elementary and Secondary Education Act (Every Student Succeeds Act [ESSA]) provides additional support and flexibility for schools and districts that serve students experiencing homelessness.

Charitable, Foundation, and Agency Grants. Many schools and districts making progress in serving their students experiencing homelessness have learned to be entrepreneurial about seeking grant funding and employ full-time professional grant writers. One of the school districts that participated in our research found that employing a grant writer paid off many times over within a short time of her joining the district staff. The person was instrumental in identifying McKinney-Vento as a possible source of funding for students in a district that, at the time, did not realize it had many students who met the federal definition of homelessness. Though resources are scarce and demand for them is high, local education agencies can secure grant funding to assist in meeting the educational needs of students experiencing homelessness in their communities. We do not say this lightly; we understand this will take time and effort on the part of school liaisons, leaders, teachers, and staff. However, this investment of time and resources will result in positive outcomes for these students and the entire school community. A few foundations that provide funding related to low-income students include the Conrad N. Hilton Foundation, Gates Foundation, Melville Charitable Trust, Bank of America Charitable Foundation, Raikes Foundation, Annie E. Casey Foundation, Campion Advocacy Fund, and Charles and Helen Schwab Foundation.

COMMUNITY COALITIONS AND PARTNERSHIPS

Most communities have government, faith-based, community, and corporate-sponsored groups and organizations engaged in the work of supporting children and families. Schools and districts can develop partnerships with these groups to find collaborative ways to meet the needs of students and families experiencing homelessness. Successful and sustainable partnerships tend to share common characteristics and strategies, including:

- Ensuring a common vision among all partners;
- Establishing structured opportunities to engage stakeholders;
- Encouraging open dialogue about challenges and solutions;
- Engaging stakeholders in the use of data;
- Creating central-office capacity to sustain community schools work; and,
- Leveraging community resources and braiding funding streams. (Blank et al., 2012, p. 12)

Schools and districts seeking to improve services for students experiencing homelessness can apply these principles. These students and their families interact with other segments of public and private services in the community; developing and nurturing partnerships between schools and community partners can improve outcomes for all stakeholder groups involved.

The district and/or school site can bring together various stakeholders within a community to discuss the process of supporting students and families. These gatherings play important functions. People come together around an area of shared interest to discuss the different ways they are working toward the same goal. These discussions enable stakeholders to learn more about the resources available in the community, which increases the likelihood that the multiple local agencies will refer students and families to other agencies. Community organizations also gain a better understanding of the role that schools play in providing services and support to students and families who are homeless. These conversations reveal overlaps in service and, more importantly, the holes that may exist. They can collaboratively explore how to address those gaps in support. Organized efforts also allow for a shared mission—even if it is somewhat broad—that moves service providers and schools out of silos and into a collective approach. The goal is to begin a *collective* conversation. Schools tend to be a key space for these efforts, especially if families or family representatives are invited. The school site is accessible to everyone.

Community coalitions and connections can also be essential in sharing information about the educational rights of students experiencing homelessness. Families and youth accessing resources within these agencies often build trusting relationships with the staff. Ensuring that these service providers know about the students' educational rights and whom to contact within the district is vital. As we mentioned in previous chapters, working with families and students early in their homeless episode decreases the impact on education. These stakeholders often assist in meeting basic needs soon after a student or family experiences a crisis. Collaboration between schools and these agencies can increase the likelihood of developing an educational plan early.

A common approach to better understanding the local community context in a collaborative manner is a practice known as *community asset mapping*. According to Taliep and Ismail (2023),

> Community mapping, also known as asset mapping, is a participatory relationship-driven method that focuses on assets and resources and promotes community engagement, networking, ownership, and sustainability. As an approach that takes advantage of a community's strengths and resources, community mapping facilitates the process of uncovering solutions. Community mapping is a sequential way of identifying, visually depicting, ranking, and mobilizing tangible and intangible community assets. There are multiple ways of mapping community resources, including participatory community-engaged mapping, online mapping (Geographic Information Systems), compiling a capacity inventory, cultural mapping, community relationship mapping, and developing an interest checklist. (pp. 823–824)

Summarizing current research, Taliep and Ismail (2023, p. 829) identify several characteristics of community asset mapping, including:

- Facilitates knowledge-making *with* communities to identify and build on their existing resources, strengths, and human capabilities
- Assists communities to regain control over their lives and reclaim their own agency
- Enhances participation
- Recognizes and foregrounds the importance of networks and relationships as assets
- Visualizes or brings to the surface community assets
- Mobilizes assets, resources, skills, and strengths of individuals and communities
- Supports and encourages leadership engagement to promote action
- Adopts an integrated participatory community-driven approach
- Helps reclaim bonds of connectedness by generating community cohesiveness, solidarity, and collaboration
- Conceives novel theoretical insights

Recognizing the strengths and expertise of community members is integral to building trust and developing sustainable relationships that focus on mutual aid. Focusing on the strengths and knowledge of the local community allows for the leveraging of school resources in tandem with community strengths and needs. While we recognize that a process that listens to and values community input requires time and resources, it will have a lasting impact on developing a strong infrastructure for schools and communities in better meeting the needs of McKinney-Vento students. Often, people experiencing homelessness are not valued for their wisdom and expertise in navigating difficult financial, institutional, and emotional situations. They can be involved in the mapping process and development of partnerships. We include a PLC activity related to community mapping at the end of this chapter.

Youth Homelessness Demonstration Program

The Youth Homelessness Demonstration Program (YHDP) is an initiative of the U.S. Department of Housing and Urban Development (HUD) created to reduce the number of youth experiencing homelessness. YHDP aims to support selected communities, including urban, suburban, and rural areas across the United States, in the development and implementation of a coordinated community approach to preventing and ending youth homelessness (NCHE, 2024). YHDP communities must convene a youth action board (YAB); bring together a wide variety of partner systems, including housing, child welfare, education, workforce development, juvenile justice and behavioral health; assess the needs of special populations at higher risk of homelessness; and create a coordinated community plan (CCP) that assesses the needs of local youth at risk of and experiencing homelessness. To date, 110 communities have been funded and supported with dedicated YHDP technical assistance through HUD and the U.S. Department of Education. Learn more about YHDP at https://www.hud.gov/hud-partners/community-yhdp

DEVELOPING COLLABORATIVE, AUTHENTIC, AND ENDURING PARTNERSHIPS

Collaborative partnerships among educators, community partners, and families can be built that recognize the strengths and assets that students and families experiencing homelessness possess. Using strengths-oriented approaches and tools as a starting point pushes back on deficit and derogatory perceptions of individuals facing homelessness. Leveraging these approaches in their collaborations, schools and community stakeholders can work together to identify needs and develop sustainable solutions to addressing both in and out of school factors that shape processes, experiences, and outcomes for students and their families (Milner et al., 2015).

Schools are integral to the communities they serve. Educators and school sites possess knowledge, networks, and logistical resources that enable them to serve as a hub for services focused on the educational, emotional, and basic needs of students and families experiencing homelessness. Collaboration with community-based organizations, mental health clinics, shelters, and other agencies creates an ecosystem of stability, safety, and care to meet students' academic, social, physical, and emotional needs (Miller, 2011; Murphy & Tobin, 2011). McKinney-Vento mandates that schools coordinate with local services agencies and programs:

> The Coordinator for Education of Homeless Children and Youths established in each State shall . . . facilitate coordination between the State educational agency, the State social services agency, and other agencies (including mental health services) to provide services to homeless children (PL 107–110; 115 STAT. 1995).

While educators within and outside of schools have expertise in particular content areas, they may not have been trained about McKinney-Vento or how to work effectively with students experiencing poverty, housing instability, and marginalization. Individuals who possess that knowledge can provide guidance to others within a collaborative partnership. Through gaining deeper understanding of the strengths these students possess as well as the challenges they navigate, the partnership can explore potential solutions from a place of empathy, humility, respect, and care.

IDENTIFYING RESEARCH PARTNERSHIPS

Educators in schools, districts, and at state-level positions may want to gather additional information to understand how the local context of homelessness influences students' educational experiences and outcomes. However, they may not have the time or resources to do so. Similarly, educators may be approached by researchers who want to conduct studies leveraging the data from the school, district, or state. Developing partnerships with external researchers can be an effective way to gather and analyze data to make informed decisions.

We encourage educators to develop clear expectations when working with research partners. In addition to ensuring that the partners abide by confidentiality guidelines, they should also offer some level of reciprocity to the educators. For example, if a research partner engages with the district-level data, they should create a practitioner-oriented report or presentation that summarizes the key insights as well as providing research-informed recommendations. These expectations should be clearly outlined before the study begins.

As part of the community mapping process, educators can explore potential research partners that exist in the local context:

- Postsecondary institutions—In addition to faculty and graduate students looking for research projects, there may be opportunities to connect with educators about doing class projects or student club activities focused on issues of importance to educators. If the local postsecondary institution has an educational master's or doctoral program, educators could reach out to the department chairs of those programs to discuss opportunities for students to leverage school, district, or state data within their thesis or dissertation work.
- Current educators—Many educators pursue graduate degrees or administrative credentials. As in the previous point, these educators could be encouraged to leverage school-, district-, or state-level data when doing their culminating projects.
- State data systems—Many states have a commission that gathers and reports on student data. Educators can reach out to these groups with specific questions. In addition, these groups may be willing to gather additional data or develop a report to support the work of educators.
- Students and families—Current students and families can also be empowered to engage in data-gathering and analysis processes. They possess experiential knowledge related to homelessness and housing insecurity in the local context. They can also be important partners in mapping the resources available and gaps in support that exist.

Where to Start as a New Homeless Liaison

An educator new to the role of homeless liaison may be wondering where to start in doing the important work of supporting students and families. We recommend considering the follow as initial steps in transitioning to this role:

- Review McKinney-Vento documents for the district, school, and state.
- Identify school personnel in the district and at school sites who have knowledge related to working with students experiencing homelessness in the district, including counselors, social workers, attendance coordinators, and Title I program officers.
- Locate the processes in place for identifying and referring students experiencing homeless to services within the district. If no process exists, develop one by drawing from the resources in this book and potentially connecting with homeless liaisons for other districts.

- Determine if there is a list of local shelters, drop-in centers, or other agencies near the school/district that provide services and support to students experiencing homelessness. This might include connecting with educators within the school sites to understand if they have developed partnerships with community members.
- Email or call the local agencies to introduce yourself and set up time to speak with the executive director or community liaison to begin discussions of possible collaborations/partnerships.
- If resources are not available or do not seem current, consider leveraging the community mapping activity at the end of the chapter.

CHAPTER CONCLUSION

This chapter focused on securing resources and forming partnerships for schools and districts seeking to improve their services for students and families experiencing homelessness. We have discussed the concepts of prolonged economic distress for communities as well as the use of community asset mapping as a tool to meet the needs of students, youth and families experiencing housing instability. Additionally, we looked at how schools and districts have combined and leveraged sources of revenue and noted the characteristics of thriving school–community partnerships. The topics and processes outlined serve to support educators, students, and their families in the identification of what is working as well as of blind spots or areas in need of improvement. Taking a coordinated and systematic approach such as community asset mapping or an inclusive, strengths-based approach such as Participatory Action Research (see the PLC activity at end of chapter) can center common areas of interest among school and community stakeholders for further awareness and understanding of student needs and for policy development.

Guiding Questions for Individual and/or Group Reflection

1. What knowledge do you currently have about the level of economic stress your community currently faces? How might members of your community experience economic stress differently? If that knowledge is limited, where might you look to become better informed?
2. What is an example of an effective organizational partnership or collaboration you have worked with in the past? What were the characteristics that made it successful?
3. Does your school district currently have a McKinney-Vento subgrant? If so, how are funds used? If not, what are the steps to submit one in the future?

4. How can your school or district identify, build, and nurture collaborative relationships with local partners?

Professional Learning Community Activities

Activity 1: Community Mapping

Schools and districts need to understand what resources exist within their community before they can build partnerships. We included a community mapping activity in Appendix G, which guides educators through the process of identifying individuals and groups within their local context who could be partners in supporting students and families experiencing homelessness.

Activity 2: Research Partnerships

Educators may have broader questions about student and family experiences than could be assessed by looking at school or district data. Educators could identify a specific question or concern that they want to explore. Then they have a few options:

- The group could leverage their expertise and develop an informal study/assessment. Educators could divide responsibility for the work. After the data are gathered, the group could assess what they have learned and develop recommendations.
- Earlier in this chapter, we provided an overview of different research partnerships that could be established. The group could reflect on the potential partnerships and then develop a plan to invite others to join the work.
- Appendix H focuses on action-oriented research that would include students and/or families. Reflect on whether and how this strategy could be useful.

CHAPTER 10

Continuing Education After High School

Most educators and policymakers focus on the challenges of students experiencing homelessness within the preschool through high school settings. Given the low high school graduation rates of these students, a focus on earning a diploma makes sense. However, earning a high school diploma alone will not allow most of these young people to achieve financial and residential stability. Over the past decade, greater attention has been given to supporting students experiencing homelessness as they transition out of high school and pursue a postsecondary degree or credential. A student's ability to pursue higher education depends upon local community resources and support provided by educators (Kull et al., 2019). Postsecondary institutions can also play a critical role in assisting with the multifaceted challenges these students endure as they apply for and transition to college (Hallett, 2010).

An important step is to normalize the idea that students experiencing homelessness *can* attend college. Several articles and books have been published recently that illustrate that individuals currently and formerly homeless attend colleges and universities across the United States (Hallett & Crutchfield, 2017). In addition, campuses have begun to develop supports to address housing and food insecurity (Hallett & Skrla, 2021). Educators can share information with students during college preparation conversations and activities to help them realize that supports exist on many campuses. Helping them realize that "students like me" go to college and succeed is essential.

While we focus on students, we want to note that these resources may also be useful for their parents or guardians. Educators may encounter a parent or guardian who wants to explore how to earn a postsecondary degree or certificate to achieve residential stability for their family. The resources in this chapter may be useful to share with them. In addition, they may want to contact community agencies and local postsecondary institutions to see if additional resources may be available for parents from low-income backgrounds. For example, many postsecondary institutions have specific programs and services for students over 25 years old.

In this chapter, we discuss what PK–12 educators can do to support students who are homeless as they navigate the postsecondary education exploration, selection, and transition processes. We begin by discussing the aspirations of students for postsecondary education and the vital role that educators play in supporting these aspirations. Then we share some resources available to assist students in preparing for and transitioning to postsecondary education.

STUDENTS PERCEIVE HIGHER EDUCATION AS PATHWAY TO STABILITY

Our research as well as that of others has consistently found that youth experiencing homelessness aspire to attend college (Hallett et al., 2019). In one of our studies, we spoke to 160 young people who were experiencing homelessness—they overwhelmingly believed that college was their only pathway to future stability (Tierney et al., 2008). For example, we worked with a student whose mother and grandmother had both been homeless throughout her life; pursuing a postsecondary degree was an attempt to break the generational poverty that her family struggled to overcome.

Although these students possess aspirations to pursue college, they attend at low rates (Skobba et al., 2018). About 15% of individuals 18–25 who have experienced homelessness attend college as compared to 52% of their peers with stable housing (Kull et al., 2019). Completing a high school diploma serves as a barrier for many of these students. However, lack of knowledge of how the higher educational process works also limits their participation. Educators play an important role in fostering aspirations by providing encouragement and information.

Many of the college students who experienced homelessness that we have worked with endured significant trauma associated with unsafe and unstable residential situations throughout their childhood. The students longed to have a stable living arrangement like the other students. Often, the students' situations were related to their parents' history of residential instability. For example, one student who couch-surfed between friends' homes while trying to complete his community college degree mentioned that he would occasionally visit his father, who lived in an alley downtown. He aspired to earn a psychology degree to help others who had similar traumatic experiences.

For the students who make it to college, attending class can provide structure that is missing from their lives. The time on campus may feel secure and predictable as compared to the uncertainty that permeates the rest of their lives (Hallett & Freas, 2018). The students spoke about how the daily structure and long-term goals helped them endure the chaos in their lives. While the journey to (and through) college may be challenging, these students need the stability and hope that postsecondary education provides.

ROLE OF PK–12 EDUCATORS IN SUPPORTING ASPIRATIONS

In this section, we highlight a few of the ways that educators can assist these students in achieving their educational goals after high school.

Encouragement

We have encountered educators who encourage students to secure residential stability *before* the students consider pursuing a postsecondary education. Taking a minimum-wage job may (or may not) enable the young person to cobble together enough money to survive, but rarely leads to long-term financial and residential stability. In addition, these messages can be discouraging to students who aspire to attend college. The students may hear a signal that college is not for them.

Educators can begin providing encouragement and information about postsecondary education as early as elementary school. Many of the students experiencing homelessness will be the first in their families to attend college. Planting the seed that college could be an option for these students early on will frame how they engage with school and the aspirations they develop. Students in elementary school do not need detailed information about the application process. However, they can begin exploring the different careers that are possible with a college degree. In addition, many local postsecondary institutions have museums or events that could serve as field trips to give students an opportunity to see themselves on a college campus. We also know of several institutions that will coordinate a campus tour for elementary schools. One of the campuses we worked with had a professor who created a "college class" that allowed elementary students to spend an hour in a lecture hall learning about science from age-appropriate experiments.

As these students progress to middle and high school, they will benefit from more specific and individual encouragement. Just hearing "I think you could go to college" can be a transformative moment for students who may not believe they could earn a postsecondary degree or credential. While having a general presentation of information in a class or assembly can enable educators to share general tips and guidance, these students often have complex situations that require a one-on-one meeting as a follow-up (Venegas & Hallett, 2008). Students also benefit from specific encouragement. For example, a student is doing well in math and may want to consider an engineering degree, or a student demonstrates success in the automotive class and may want to explore the technical certificate program at the local community college.

Dual Enrollment and Advanced Placement

Students can begin their college coursework while in high school. For students experiencing homelessness, this can be a cost-effective way of getting college-level classes completed. In addition, some postsecondary institutions will accept Advanced Placement (AP) classes or exams as college credit. High-achieving students and/or those with parents who have knowledge about the importance of dual enrollment or AP coursework are most likely to spot and take advantage of these opportunities. Educators can ensure that all students have this information and create pathways for their participation.

While some high schools offer the dual enrollment classes at the local high school during the typical school day, others require the students to travel to the community college. For students who are homeless or highly mobile, transportation to the local community college may be challenging. Educators can work with the district offices and community college administration to explore transportation options. For example, some cities provide a free bus pass for college students, or the district may offer a bus if a certain number of students enroll. There also may be online course options if transportation proves to be a barrier (see Appendix F).

College Support Programming and Campus Visits

Students experiencing homelessness benefit from access to college preparation activities. College preparation programs, such as Advancement via Individual Determination (AVID) and TRIO, provide college information to students from low-income backgrounds and those who will be the first in their family to attend college. These programs also connect students with teachers and mentors who serve as guides through the college preparation and transition processes. The Higher Education Opportunity Act of 2008 increased access to the federal TRIO programs for youth experiencing homelessness, which includes Talent Search, Equal Opportunity Centers, and Upward Bound programs. This Act automatically makes students in homeless situations eligible for TRIO. For GEAR-UP programs not using a cohort model, the Act encourages these programs to include youth experiencing homelessness as a priority.

The federal revisions of ESSA require the homeless liaison to work with the high schools to assist with providing college information and support. Educators can collaborate with the homeless liaison to develop programming and opportunities at their school sites. These programs do not need to be separate from other college preparation activities; however, there may be specific questions or concerns that students experiencing homelessness have about how to prepare and what resources may be available.

ESSA also requires states to develop a plan for how these students will gain access to advising and preparation to increase college readiness. These are important steps. However, the federal government has not created a comprehensive policy to encourage success once students enter college that would be comparable to what McKinney-Vento does at the PK–12 level.

Educators who coordinate college preparation programs in middle or high school should reflect on how students are selected for these opportunities and ensure that students experiencing homelessness are included. In addition, these educators can intentionally include resources and information within the programs that specifically benefit these students. By including these resources within the college preparation curriculum, educators send a clear message that students experiencing homelessness will be supported in college and encourage them to continue to pursue their aspirations.

Fee Waivers for Exams and Applications

Most 4-year institutions require students to submit either ACT or SAT scores as part of the application process. Both testing programs have fee waivers available for students from low-income backgrounds. The student must be in 11th or 12th grade and demonstrate one of several indicators of low-income status. The request must be submitted through a high school counselor. While the waivers do not explicitly cover youth experiencing homelessness, most will be eligible due to low-income status.

The college application process involves several costs. The College Board recommends that students apply to several institutions to increase the likelihood of getting accepted as well as to give students choices once financial aid packages get sent from each institution. While a few have free applications, most colleges and universities have fees that range from $25 to $100. Applying to 6–8 institutions can easily cost $300 to $400. For a student and family without residential stability, these costs can exceed monthly income. College application fee waivers exist from the College Board and the National Association of College Admissions Counseling (NACAC). Students who demonstrate financial need can receive up to 4 fee waivers from both College Board and NACAC, which would cover the cost of 8 college applications. In addition, students can contact a postsecondary institution's admissions office to request that the application fee be waived.

Advanced Placement (AP) exams can be useful for students attempting to demonstrate academic competence. These exams cost approximately $100 each. Students enrolled in the federal free and reduced lunch program are eligible for a fee waiver from the College Board to reduce the cost. Most states and some school districts have additional fee waiver programs to reduce or eliminate the costs of AP exams. These programs often have a limited number of waivers available. While no explicit provisions may exist for youth experiencing homelessness, most will meet the eligibility requirements.

College Transition Plans

The end of high school marks an important transition point. For students experiencing homelessness, school may have been the most stable aspect of their lives. Ending the familiar routine can be scary—especially if these young people do not have a clear plan and guidance on how to successfully transition to the next stage of life.

Constructing a college transition plan with students enables them to develop a concrete plan with the necessary information to succeed. Transition plans have previously been used to support students with disabilities or those in the foster care system. For example, the federal government requires all students with disabilities to develop a transition plan as part of their final Individual Education Plan (IEP) before graduating from high school.

While not currently required by law, we encourage educators to work with students experiencing homelessness to develop a transition plan before they exit high school (see the PLC activity at the end of the chapter; Hallett & Woelki, 2025). The first stage could occur at the start of 11th grade or earlier to support students in beginning to explore their options after high school. The second stage could occur during the final year of high school when students need to make final decisions about next steps. We argue for the importance of creating transition plans for students experiencing homelessness (Woelki et al., 2025). However, for educators who work in high-poverty schools, they may want to integrate the transition planning process into the general curriculum for all students.

CHOOSING A COLLEGE, UNIVERSITY, OR TRADE SCHOOL

Selecting a college is complex. Students have many options, ranging from short-term credential programs (e.g., an electrician or cosmetology certificate) to community and technical colleges to 4-year institutions. Most of these programs require individuals to apply and, if accepted, pay the cost of tuition. Individuals also need to assess which degree or certificate program would be a good fit for their goals. Although most low-income and first-generation college students may not be clear on this, not all postsecondary degree and certificate programs are the same, and some predatory institutions target vulnerable student populations. For students who may experience significant challenges completing high school, many community and technical colleges have options for students to pursue postsecondary education without earning a diploma.

After selecting the institution(s) that would be a good fit, the student then needs to apply for and secure funding to cover the costs. Often, deadlines must be met to be considered for acceptance, and prospective students may have to take an exam (e.g., ACT or SAT) as part of the application process for a 4-year degree program. The students experiencing homeless situations whom we have worked with speak about the challenges of navigating all these requirements while also meeting their basic needs. Given that participation in after-school programs can be difficult for some students, they recommend having this information integrated into the general course content. For example, a portion of the homeroom meeting could be dedicated to college preparation.

Students experiencing homelessness often have needs that differ from their housed peers. In addition to finding a postsecondary program that aligns with their goals, they also need to meet more immediate needs. These students benefit from housing offered by postsecondary institutions. Part of the college exploration process should include considering housing options that may be available on campus or within the community surrounding the postsecondary institution. Students should not become discouraged if an institution does not have housing or if the on-campus housing appears expensive—the financial aid package that the student receives will include both cost of tuition and other expenses, including books, food, and housing. If the student is concerned about costs, they should reach out to the college's financial aid or admissions office to ask questions and get advice. For students who feel uncomfortable or ill-equipped to ask questions, an educator may want to join the call to assist.

For the most part, earning a high school diploma is a prerequisite to pursuing higher education. However, students who do not complete a diploma still have options. They may attend adult school to complete the requirements for a diploma or GED. Most states allow individuals to attend community college even if they did not earn a diploma. Students choosing this option may complete the diploma as part of their coursework or could earn a technical certificate (e.g., automotive repair, plumbing) that would give them career options.

RESOURCES TO COVER TUITION

Students experiencing homelessness have multiple funding options to pursue. We begin by discussing the application process for federal aid, which is required for most need-based loans, grants and scholarships. We then provide an overview of other scholarships and grants.

Free Application for Federal Student Aid

All students seeking federal grants and loans must complete the Free Application for Federal Student Aid (FAFSA). The application requires students to report the earnings and tax information of parents or guardians. Students who are homeless and highly mobile may have a difficult time gaining access to this information for a variety of reasons. Some homeless youth no longer have connections with their parents and live unaccompanied. In addition, frequent mobility may result in lost documents. Homeless liaisons are responsible for ensuring that unaccompanied youth know their rights concerning independent status for FAFSA. In the sections that follow, we highlight special considerations for subgroups of students experiencing homelessness.

Unaccompanied Youth. The College Cost Reduction and Access Act (CCRAA) (2007) provides opportunities for unaccompanied youth who are homeless to declare independent status on the FAFSA. To understand the implications of this policy, three terms need to be unpacked: unaccompanied, homeless, and independent. An *unaccompanied* youth is not under the care of a parent or legal guardian. Unaccompanied youth may have complicated relationships with parents—requiring parent information may exclude them from college. *Homeless,* within this provision, appears to be a bit more narrowly defined. Students living doubled-up would most often not be considered because this residential arrangement typically involves being with a parent or guardian. *Independent* refers to the filing status of the FAFSA. Students who qualify for independent status do not need to include parent or guardian tax information. This may increase the amount of grants and other need-based support.

To qualify as independent, the young person must have been unaccompanied and homeless within the 12-month period beginning the July before graduation. The policy also extends the protections to young people who are at significant risk of becoming homeless, for example, if the student has received an eviction notice. Students must be in high school when submitting the FAFSA and be 21 years of age or younger. This extended time frame allows for students who may take longer to complete a diploma to still qualify for CCRAA protections. At the age of 24, students applying to or enrolled in undergraduate education automatically qualify for independent status. Therefore, CCRAA creates a two-year period at the ages of 22 and 23 when these students are not explicitly eligible for independent status; however, these students can still appeal for independent status directly through the postsecondary institution's financial aid office.

The typical process for determining independent status involves three general steps. First, the student submits the FAFSA application as an independent student. Financial aid offices at the postsecondary institutions then make a final determination of eligibility. The second step involves students submitting a letter to the institution's financial aid office that outlines their situation. Based upon this letter and a student interview, institutions can verify eligibility. However, most institutions require third-party verification. The third step involves verification and can be completed by a district homeless liaison, high school counselor, administrator, teacher, community member, or other individuals who know about the student's situation. While it is not preferred, a family member can also serve as the third-party verification. Using this information, the postsecondary institution determines if the student will be classified as independent for the purposes of financial aid. If a student is determined to be ineligible, an appeal can be submitted. Unfortunately, many postsecondary institutions do not clearly articulate how the appeal process works, and students may assume that an appeal is futile. This is when they may need an advocate to negotiate the process.

The review process must be completed each academic year. Some postsecondary institutions draw from the previously submitted materials and require the student only to submit the personal statement. However, the student should be prepared to submit third-party verification each year. For those who used a PK–12 educator when initially submitting the appeal, it may be difficult for them to return to the same person to get verification. The students may not have a continued relationship with the school district personnel and even if they do, the educator may not be familiar with the students' living situation to verify homelessness. When working with students during the initial year of submission, educators should begin brainstorming with the student to identify someone who will provide third-party verification in subsequent years. For example, the student may be encouraged to continue a relationship with the homeless liaison or high school counselor; however, a backup plan might be needed if that person changes positions over the 4-to-5-year period that the student is in college.

Accompanied Youth. Since CCRAA does not explicitly cover those youth who are accompanied by a parent or guardian, the process differs. Most youth who experience homelessness while living with a parent or guardian will qualify for need-based grants and scholarships. Given that a family does not have the financial means to achieve residential stability, the FAFSA application will typically result in an assumption that the parent or guardian cannot financially assist the student. For all intents and purposes, this would result in a similar financial package as that for an unaccompanied student who achieved independent status. If parental or guardian tax information is easily accessible, the student should process the FAFSA application without the appeal. If a circumstance exists that makes it difficult or unsafe to secure parental tax information, the student should follow the same procedures for applying as an unaccompanied student. In these cases, the student should work closely with the college financial aid office and explain their residential situation to ensure that the financial aid advisor has a complete picture of the student's situation. They may grant the appeal and process the student as independent.

Federal, State, and Institutional Grants

Grants are funding that students do not need to repay. The federal Pell Grant amount is determined as part of the FAFSA application process. For the 2023–2024 academic year, the Pell Grant provided a maximum of $7,395 per year for up to four years of undergraduate education. The exact amount depends upon factors such as cost of tuition and full-time enrollment. Students can also appeal the decision if they do not receive a Pell Grant.

Several states offer need-based grants, which most students experiencing homelessness would be eligible to receive. For example, the State Need-based Grant in South Carolina provides up to $1,500 per semester, and the

Pennsylvania State Grant provides up to $5,260 per year. The requirements and processes vary. Some states require students to submit a separate application, which may or may not be based solely upon financial need. The high school guidance counselor and local college financial aid office have information about state grants.

Many institutions also provide need-based grants. Typically, the institution determines eligibility while reviewing the FAFSA information and developing the student's financial aid package. For example, the University of Nebraska system waives tuition for students whose family has a combined income of less than $65,000 a year and meet a few academic requirements.

Scholarships

There are many community and national scholarship programs; they often require students to write essays that involve sharing their story. Most postsecondary institutions also have scholarships available for students. Students need to fill out a supplemental application with the institution's financial aid office. The institution uses this application to determine if a student is eligible for the multiple different scholarships that they have available to distribute. Some of these scholarships, too, may require a personal essay or letter.

The process of writing these essays can be difficult for students who have endured trauma. Students may not understand why a funder is asking for personal information. They also may not feel comfortable sharing embarrassing and vulnerable moments. These students may not want to relive their trauma to get a scholarship.

Educators can help students understand the process. Explaining why an institution or funder is asking for the student to share their experiences may be helpful. An educator can guide the student through writing an essay in a way that conveys the student's experiences to meet qualifications for the funding without further traumatizing them. Not all details need to be included to convey the student's need.

Scholarships for Students in Homeless Situations

There are a few scholarships specifically dedicated to support postsecondary education for students experiencing homelessness. Local organizations may have additional scholarship opportunities. In addition, educators may connect with the postsecondary institutions their students plan to attend. They may have institutional scholarships that specifically support this population but are not easy to find.

The National Association for the Education of Homeless Children and Youth (NAEHCY) offers a minimum of two scholarships each year to students who have experienced homelessness. The applicant must have experienced homelessness at some point during PK–12 schooling and demonstrate average or above average achievement. For a full list of the qualifications and the application, please visit the website: https://naehcy.org/scholars/scholarship-applicants/

Although not specifically designated for homelessness, scholarship programs targeting low-income and first-generation college students can be worth pursuing. A few examples include the Horatio Alger Scholarship Program (https://scholars.horatioalger.org) and the Coca Cola Scholarship Program (www.coca-colascholarsfoundation.org).

Loans

Students can receive loans to cover the cost of their education. The college will determine the student's eligibility while developing the financial aid package. Before accepting loans, the student should meet with a college financial aid office to ensure they understand the process. In addition, a PK–12 educator or trusted member of the local community may want to review the financial aid package with the student. This is important to ensure that they do not sign a contract with a predatory company.

TRANSITIONING TO POSTSECONDARY EDUCATION

The transition to a postsecondary institution can be challenging for students experiencing homelessness (Hallett et al., 2019). The summer after high school and the first academic term of postsecondary education tend to be the most important time periods when high school educators offer support. The number of students who have been accepted to a postsecondary institution and plan to attend at the end of high school slowly decreases during the summer months—typically called "summer melt." According to Castleman and Page (2013), "Nearly 40% of students intending on a community college and nearly 20% of students intending on a four-year institution fail to matriculate in the fall after high school" (p. 212).

Many critical things happen during the summer months before college begins. For example, classes are selected and financial aid packages become final. Most postsecondary institutions require placement exams for math and English before a student can register for classes. Four-year institutions require housing deposits and orientation. Emails and mailings are sent to students from the postsecondary institutions with firm deadlines for response. While progress has been made in simplifying these documents, they still can be confusing for students. Some colleges have a single point of contact to coordinate services and provide individual support for students experiencing homelessness (Hallett et al., 2018). This person may be a valuable resource to leverage as students transition to college. The National Association for the Education of Homeless Children and Youth developed a guide to practitioners who do this work which is free on their website—the *SPOC User Guide* (Havlik, 2024).

To complicate the matter, students in homeless situations may not have a consistent residential address and may have limited access to the internet while school is not in session. Further, they rarely have access to high school teachers and counselors who could answer questions, since school is not in session. While the wait may be only 2 or 3 months, students experiencing homelessness may need to focus on meeting basic needs and may feel responsible for helping families survive. The fear of the unknown can lead students to change their minds at the last minute, particularly if they do not have access to a mentor who can answer questions and provide encouragement. Some high schools offer stipends for high school counselors to provide college counseling during the summer months.

Some community colleges and universities offer summer bridge programs in the weeks leading up to the fall term. The design of these programs varies from an extended orientation for a few days before class to a month-long program that involves earning college credit. These programs can assist low-income and first-generation college students through the transition to college. In addition, most of the programs at 4-year institutions offer housing.

For students in homeless situations moving onto campus or out of the local area, getting their things to the campus can be challenging. We worked with a young man who did not know how to get his three bags of things 20 miles across the city to move into the residence hall. In working with a mentor, he figured out a public transportation plan that enabled him to arrive at UCLA by city bus. He discussed how embarrassed he was to arrive on campus with three trash bags that contained everything he owned while most of his peers were unpacking items specifically purchased for their dorm room from their parents' SUVs. For students experiencing homelessness who may need to travel to another city or state, the cost of transportation may be prohibitive. These students may need guidance planning ahead for travel expenses as well as connecting with the postsecondary institution to explore potential financial support.

A few states have provisions that address some of the concerns for college students in homeless situations. California, for example, passed AB1228, which allows students experiencing homelessness under the age of 25 to get priority housing and housing during breaks. The homeless liaison should work with the state director to get information about the state-level policies related to college access and success. This information can then be shared with the educators and staff members on-site to ensure that students know about the resources available.

Although steps have been taken to increase college access for youth experiencing homelessness and residential instability, NAEHCY (2013) encourages educators and advocates to consider a few additional steps. Students in homeless situations will likely need support negotiating housing while in college. For those who choose to attend an institution without student housing, careful planning will be needed to achieve residential stability while in college. And for those students who choose to live in on-campus housing, they will need to work with the campus housing program to ensure that they have a place to stay during breaks, when residential halls often close. The second recommendation involves increasing employment opportunities for these students who may need to work while in college. Third, the students may need assistance figuring out transportation to campus if living off-campus. Relatedly, they may need help planning and financing the move to another move or state to begin college. Finally, these students may need access to tutoring and academic support services. Given the negative impact that residential instability has on academic achievement, these students may need academic support services to make the transition to college coursework. For example, DePaul University has a year-round housing assistance program that includes many forms of additional support for students selected into the Dax Program. And the Massachusetts Department of Higher Education creates resources and funding to assist the state's postsecondary institutions in implementing many of these recommendations.

OSU Emergency Food Pantry

Oregon State University attempts to address the issue of food insecurity on campus by supporting a food pantry. Twice a month, students can come to the pantry to receive food. The project works in collaboration with the local food bank. The campus has found that locating the resource on campus increases the likelihood that students will take advantage of this resource because the pantry has become just another resource on campus.

Students in homeless situations may have limited access to these college preparation activities if there are strict GPA requirements. Residential instability significantly impacts educational achievement. Any movement between schools also limits access to teachers who would nominate students to participate in these programs. As such, most individuals who are homeless and highly mobile do not gain access to these important resources and network connections. Finding ways for these students to access college preparation resources is essential. We encourage all teachers to integrate conversations about college into course content to help students learn about the college preparation processes.

CHAPTER CONCLUSION

Schools play an important role in preparing students for college. For students in homeless situations, most of whom would be first-generation college students, educators serve as vital sources of knowledge about college access. While efforts to improve high school graduation need to continue, students experiencing homelessness would greatly benefit from college access preparation. For many, their long-term stability depends on it.

Guiding Questions for Individual and/or Group Reflection

1. What college access programming exists in your school and district? Has there been a review of the application policies in terms of how youth in homeless situations are integrated into the programming? What additional opportunities might be created?
2. What community partners exist in your area that could assist with college access? These could include community colleges, universities, community organizations, mentoring programs, and advocates. How could the school and district build partnerships with these entities to increase postsecondary opportunities for youth experiencing homelessness?
3. How could the school or district connect with postsecondary institutions to ease the transition for youth without residential stability? These institutions often have personnel whose job is to make these connections. Do people in your school know who the contacts with local college universities, and trade schools are?

Professional Learning Community Activities

Activity 1: Transition Plan

Students should begin the college preparation process *at least* 2 years prior to graduating from high school, especially for students experiencing homelessness. There are several things that students need to do starting their junior year to ensure that they are adequately prepared to submit applications, secure financial aid, and transition to college. We encourage educators to consider developing a formal process of supporting students experiencing homelessness. The ecology of promise framework could be leveraged to explore ways to offer holistic, proactive, developmental, and strengths-oriented support, which includes collaborating with educators in different roles and organizations.

A free college transition plan template is available to provide guidance for educators and students on how to prepare for colleges their final 2 years of high school. (This tool could be integrated into the programming for all students.)

Educators should review the transition tool and support materials. We also encourage schools and districts to consider drawing this information and individualizing templates that reflect the needs, experiences, and goals of your students as well as the resources available in your schools, district and community.

Begin by reviewing the following resources (scan the QR codes):

- How could the tool be used by the school and/or community partners?
- Are there aspects of the tool that need to be adapted to meet the needs of the local or state context?
- Develop a plan for piloting the tool and/or integrating it within current college preparation programming.

Activity 2: Map Resources Available

To support students in making decisions about pursuing a postsecondary degree or certificate, educators need a clear understanding of what options are available. At times, this information exists within a school but may not be shared with all the educators on campus. Since students may build connections with different educators, the information should be distributed broadly.

Educators should explore what postsecondary opportunities and resources exist within the local community. We recognize that some rural communities may have limited local options, so they need to explore options further away from the school. We encourage you to reflect on how the ecology of promise approach can inform this process. In creating a postsecondary opportunity map, consider the following:

1. Identify the postsecondary preparation resources available for students:
   a. Does the school offer college preparation programming during or after school? If so, what process exists to ensure that students experiencing homelessness have access to these programs? If not, could the school develop a program that could be integrated into the coursework for all students?
   b. Does the local community have college preparation supports available? If so, what exists, and how would students gain

access to these programs? If not, is there a partner who may be interested in creating a program for students?

c. Do the local college campuses offer college preparation resources or programs? If so, what exists (e.g., college tours, bridge programs, college preparation mentoring, assistance with college applications, etc.)? Do the campuses have specific resources for students who are low-income and/or homeless? If programming does not exist, would the local college be open to creating resources or opportunities for students?
d. Does the local community college offer dual enrollment opportunities? If so, how could the school partner with the college to increase opportunities for all students, also addressing the specific needs of those who are experiencing homelessness?
e. Does the district homeless liaison or state coordinator have information and/or resources to support the postsecondary aspirations of students experiencing homelessness?

2. Identify the postsecondary campuses and programs in the local community and/or region:
    a. List the postsecondary campuses that exist, including technical and community colleges as well as 4-year universities. In addition to the campuses with a physical presence in the community, educators may also want to consider what online programs may be available for students.
    b. Identify the supports, including housing, basic needs, and other resources, that each campus can make available for students experiencing homelessness.
3. Identify the funding sources available:
    a. Does the state offer grants or scholarships for students from low-income backgrounds?
    b. What local scholarships exist for students from low-income backgrounds?
    c. Do the local campuses offer grants or scholarships for students from low income backgrounds?
    d. Do the local community and/or campuses offer resources and support related to completing the FAFSA?
    e. While grants and scholarships rarely focus on homelessness, educators should explore whether there are specific grants or scholarships available for these students.
4. Integrate information into programming:
    a. How could all educators (e.g., teachers, leaders, and staff in all positions) be made aware of the postsecondary resources and information gathered?

b. How could postsecondary resources and support be integrated into programming for all students? Are there additional ways that students experiencing homelessness could get support specific to their needs?
c. How could district homeless liaisons and state coordinators integrate the information into their programming?
d. How could families and community partners be provided access to the information and resources gathered? Are there opportunities to strengthen partnerships to support these students' postsecondary goals?

CHAPTER 11

Continued Learning and Professional Development for Educators

Educators are lifelong learners who recognize the importance of continuing to explore ways to integrate effective strategies into their practice. They also tend to be keenly aware that local, state, and national contexts evolve and change. For example, the demographics of a school site may change significantly over time; practices and policies that had previously been effective may need re-imagining. Teachers who began teaching in the 1990s would not have imagined the need for policies related to smartphones and artificial intelligence. We encourage continued learning and engagement beyond the issues we highlight as contexts evolve.

In this chapter, we provide guidance on how to extend and expand learning beyond what was presented in this book. We begin with the context challenges that underscore the importance of continued learning. One-off professional development opportunities rarely have sustained impact because the context changes over time. We then move to explore opportunities to extend learning beyond what has been presented thus far. The final activities prompt educators to formulate a professional development plan.

REASONS TO CONTINUE LEARNING AND ENGAGING

Educators reading this final chapter likely have implemented many of the recommendations presented and may be seeing positive results. We affirm that work. We also want to name the contextual challenges that justify continued learning and engagement related to supporting students experiencing homelessness.

Educator Turnover

The teacher turnover rate is high, especially in high-needs schools. According to Ronfeldt et al. (2013, p. 5),

> Teacher turnover rates can be high, particularly in schools serving low income, non-White, and low-achieving student populations. Nationally, about 30% of new teachers leave the profession within 5 years, and the turnover rate is about 50% higher in high-poverty schools as compared to more affluent ones (Darling-Hammond & Sykes, 2003; Ingersoll, 2001, 2003; ERS, 2024). Teacher turnover rates also tend to be higher in urban and lower-performing schools (Hanushek, Kain, & Rivkin, 1999).

In addition to the impact rapid turnover has on student achievement in general, teacher turnover also affects other aspects of school operations, including professional development. For example, a school or district that implements professional development on McKinney-Vento, ESSA, or services for students experiencing homelessness during one school year may find that within 5 years, half of the teaching staff who had the training will no longer be at that school if it is in a high-needs area (Allensworth et al., 2009). Similar turnover rates exist for school support staff and school leaders. Any plan for professional development about McKinney-Vento, ESSA, and serving students and families experiencing homelessness needs to be a plan for continuous annual training. The issue must be kept in the foreground and integrated into the fabric of normal school practices.

Changes in Local Context

Communities evolve over time. For example, a school serving middle-class families with a low rate of homelessness may see an influx of families living doubled-up during a recession, as happened to many schools between 2008 and 2010. Or a shelter for students experiencing homelessness may open. Or the district may realign the school boundaries. Or any number of changes may slowly or quickly alter the student population of a school or district. Educators who continue to engage with learning and explore data will be better equipped to proactively respond to these changes in ways that support student experiences and outcomes.

Shifts in National and State Policy

While the general protections within the McKinney-Vento Act have existed for decades, the specifics have changed over time. The federal policies have been refined with each reauthorization, and the amount of federal funding dedicated to implementing McKinney-Vento is determined each year. Educators need to remain updated on the federal requirements and guidelines. Similarly, each state interprets the federal guidelines and, in some cases, adds protections that must be implemented within the state. Federal funding for the McKinney-Vento Act is funneled through state departments of education. Each state determines the requirements and processes for districts and school sites to access those funds. These policies and processes change over time.

Complexity of the Issue

Homelessness and housing insecurity are complex issues that rarely can be solved by schools alone. Educators may decide to focus on a specific issue during one academic year (e.g., improving the identification system or building community partnerships) and then build upon that accomplishment in subsequent years. Schools and districts must not get overwhelmed by the magnitude of the issue, but instead plan for continuous learning and action.

Educators may also need to continue developing partnerships with community partners and organizations to learn about the local context of homelessness and housing insecurity and to provide training for those partners about the educational context. Specific educational stakeholders who may need training include homeless liaisons, Title I coordinators, McKinney-Vento state coordinators, site leaders, site office personnel, teachers, case managers, school-based social workers, and homeless shelter staff. Other less obvious school staff such as food service workers and school resource officers (SROs) should also be considered and included in schoolwide training on McKinney-Vento. There are many overlapping issues, but training may need to be differentiated based upon each role.

OPPORTUNITIES

Many resources exist for educators to engage in continued learning related to supporting students and families experiencing homelessness. We provide a few ideas to help guide the planning process; however, we also encourage educators to explore other resources. For those engaged in a professional learning community, we recommend keeping a list of questions that come up in your meetings. These questions can be useful in narrowing the focus for next steps.

Theory of Action

School leaders planning professional development focused on services for students experiencing homelessness should think about how the development activities they provide will lead to the changes they wish to see in the schools and districts. In other words, leaders need a coherent *theory of action* that guides their planning and delivery of professional learning opportunities for all stakeholder groups. Prior research on effective professional development has revealed some ideas about what such a theory of action might look like. In considering how to design school-wide and/or district-wide ongoing professional development on school services for students and families experiencing homelessness, high mobility, and residential instability, the content knowledge, opportunities for active learning (as opposed to sit-and-get sessions where the "expert" presenter simply talks at a passive audience), and integration with other professional learning should be at the forefront of design and delivery decisions (Garet et al., 2001).

Teachers, administrators, homeless liaisons, Title I coordinators, front office staff, parent groups, food service and facilities staff, counselors, and others involved in working with students experiencing homelessness benefit from robust professional development that includes guidance related to action. What we suggest goes far beyond a typical isolated in-service session that presents basic facts with little or no follow-up, suggestions for implementation, or evaluation. Schools benefit from collaborating with local community organizations to build relationships that can fill the gaps and meet the subsistence and well-being needs of students and families experiencing housing instability. Movement toward a coherent, sustainable program of professional development could begin with a self-assessment of current professional development programming within schools and districts.

Collaborations With Community Agencies

McKinney-Vento is an educational policy that serves to support the educational needs of students experiencing housing instability. Housing instability impacts students and families in significant ways well beyond the school setting. We want to first recognize that most liaisons are already overburdened with many other roles and responsibilities. We discussed partnerships and collaborations in Chapter 9; we include a brief discussion here to recognize that at least part of the professional development administered by schools should include local community organizations who provide housing, food and other basic needs to students and families facing housing instability. Gaining an understanding of local services available to students can, in the long run, free up time, resources, and energy of liaisons. Finally, supplying students and families with connections to basic needs that impact academic performance, but are beyond what schools can provide, can create lasting support and relationships between schools and the local community.

Expanding the Learning Group

The initial stage of learning may involve a school site, district-level staff, or state-level coordination team. The conclusion of that learning process may lead to the recognition that additional insights and action could emerge by expanding the learning network. For example:

- An entire school feeder pattern from preschool through high school could develop a professional development opportunity to review and revise how students and families experiencing homelessness navigate the entire educational process.
- The community mapping process may evolve into an opportunity to learn and collaborate with multiple partners in the local context, which could begin with a shared learning process, goal-setting, and action plan.
- The state coordinator may invite district homeless liaisons and/or site-level points of contact in a collaborative learning process that involves elevating effective practices and reimagining those that have been less effective.
- Schools at the same level (e.g., two elementary schools) may develop a partnership to learn from each other and share promising practices.

Deepening Learning Through Teaching or Training

Educators will gain valuable insights by engaging with the materials and activities presented in this book as well as by building upon our recommendations in ways that reflect the needs of their students and local community. Identifying those key insights and sharing them with other educators provides opportunities to deepen individual learning and to assist others in the learning process. The process may also lead to developing additional partnerships and learning from their experiences. While multiple opportunities exist to share insights with other educators, here are a few ideas:

- Identify local, regional, or national conferences to share what was learned and materials that were developed. Many district-, county-, or state-level McKinney-Vento professional development trainings exist. Educators could propose a presentation or workshop that highlights a key insight, tool, or process that emerged from their work.
- The local community may have a task force or group that focuses on addressing homelessness, but these groups may not focus on the role of educators. A school or district team could request an opportunity to share their work and explore potential partnerships with the group.
- Several magazines, journals, and newsletters exist for teachers, administrators, and other educators. These publications frequently highlight promising practices. A short reflection on practice could be written for these spaces.
- Media (e.g., podcasts, newspapers, TV news, and radio) outlets can be a way to share successes with a broader audience and potentially invite others to join the collaboration. Also, many news stories related to

homelessness tend to be negative or sad—sharing successes can start to shift the narrative and prompt more people to join the work.

Identify an Aspect of Learning to Gain Deeper Knowledge

As educators engage in the learning process, they may recognize ideas, issues, or challenges they want to dig deeper into understanding. For example, developing a strengths-oriented approach may sound like a great idea, but educators are uncertain what that could look like. In this case, they may want to explore Yosso's (2005) Community Cultural Wealth framework to understand the multiple assets that students and families possess—in addition to the research article cited here, there are videos, briefs, and other resources online that explain this framework. We encourage educators to approach the learning and action process with curiosity. If an initial effort or initiative does not work, seek to understand why and adjust accordingly.

Resources for Professional Development

When considering what type of content knowledge is needed for a stakeholder group in a particular phase of professional learning about issues surrounding homelessness in schools, various sources of expert knowledge are increasingly available to school leaders and others working to design such learning opportunities. Federal, state, and local organizations, databases, and clearinghouses are good sources of information, as are peer organizations that have developed effective practices of their own.

At the national level, the following organizations maintain websites that house a wealth of information that can be useful for professional development:

- Homeless and Housing Resource Center (a program of the U.S. Department of Health and Human Services Substance Abuse & Mental Health Services Administration, Center for Mental Health Services): https://hhrctraining.org/about https://www.samhsa.gov/communities/homelessness-programs-resources
- Family and Youth Services Bureau (Department of Health and Human Services): https://acf.gov/fysb/programs
- National Center for Homeless Education (The U.S. Department of Education's technical assistance site): https://nche.ed.gov/resources/
- National Association for the Education of Homeless Children and Youth (a membership organization dedicated to improving education for children and youth experiencing homelessness): http://www.naehcy.org/
- National Center on Family Homelessness (Part of the American Institutes for Research; authors of the America's Youngest Outcasts

report): https://www.air.org/centers/national-center-family-homelessness
- SchoolHouse Connection: https://schoolhouseconnection.org/

Additionally, most state departments of education offer guidance for state-level requirements and supplement resources provided by the national organizations. Several examples of these are:

- California: http://www.cde.ca.gov/sp/hs/
- Illinois: http://www.isbe.net/homeless/
- Texas: https://tea.texas.gov/texas-schools/support-for-at-risk-schools-and-students /
- Florida: https://www.fldoe.org/policy/federal-edu-programs/title-ix-mvp/
- New York: http://www.nysteachs.org/

Along with national and state official resources, a variety of organizations and foundations also provide information that can be useful for professional development. Some examples of such groups are:

- Early Childhood Technical Assistance Center (University of North Carolina at Chapel Hill): https://ectacenter.org/portal/ecdata.asp
- RAND Corporation: http://www.rand.org/topics/homelessness.html
- National Alliance to End Homelessness: http://www.endhomelessness.org/
- Ed Research for Action: https://edresearchforaction.com/

Numerous local exemplars of effective practice also exist that can serve as invaluable "existence proofs" illustrating effective and innovative ways to craft practices and partnerships that meet the educational needs of students and families experiencing housing instability. Some of these examples receive national and international press attention, and others do not. However, incorporating real-life examples of the type of schooling models one is hoping to promote is a highly effective component of transformative learning—it serves to disrupt the stable understanding that many people carry with them that not much can be done to improve educational services for students experiencing homelessness, high mobility, and residential instability. A few examples of sites with stories of improved practices include:

- Washington High School in Washington, NC, where student government leaders worked with administrators to establish food and clothing pantries that allow high school students to shop anonymously for needed items.

- Jennings School District in the St. Louis, MO, area, where the superintendent established a coalition to start the district's own homeless shelter.
- Transitional Learning Center in Stockton, CA, where children K–6 from local homeless shelters benefit from a 5:1 student–teacher ratio to receive intensive support in reading along with mental, physical, and dental health care and nutrition services.
- Joining Forces for Families in Madison, WI, where a coalition has worked to develop a community-embedded response to the challenges of poverty, including residential instability.

In these and numerous other places, schools and community partners have worked to create alternative practices that better serve the educational needs of children and families dealing with homelessness. Having exemplars, particularly local examples, of more effective practice can be a highly useful part of professional development for stakeholders on McKinney-Vento and other issues related to schooling and homelessness.

CHAPTER CONCLUSION

In the chapter, we have discussed the need for and design of professional development for stakeholder groups on the issues facing students and families who are highly mobile, residentially unstable, and homeless (see Appendix I for additional activities). The need for coherence and sustainability of such professional development has been emphasized along with the inclusion of multiple stakeholder groups beyond the small handful of school personnel typically tasked with serving this population of students. Moreover, sustainability efforts that include relationships with local community stakeholders and organizations are also key to professional development and effective implementation of McKinney-Vento. Examples and resources have been provided for schools and districts interested in improving their professional development programs about serving students and families experiencing homelessness.

Guiding Questions for Individual and/or Group Reflection

1. Have you participated in professional development related to McKinney-Vento, ESSA, Title I, or education for students experiencing homelessness? If so, how would you rate its effectiveness? What steps or activities resulted from the professional development? Have there been any resulting changes in policy, procedure, and/or practice? How would you rate the sustainability of any new practices?

2. What type of professional development do you feel would be useful for you and/or others? Who would be able to design and approve that training? What steps need to be taken to get that professional development implemented?
3. Do you know of any local exemplars of classrooms/schools/districts/organizations that are engaged in highly effective practice for the education of students experiencing homelessness? If not, how might you use research skills and professional networks to identify some?
4. Have you had any prior experience with transformative learning (whether or not that was the name applied)? Was there a learning experience that fundamentally and permanently changed the ways in which you understood and approached an issue or problem?
5. What are 2–3 steps your school or district can take to improve the identification, support, and retention of students experiencing homelessness?

Professional Learning Community Activities

Activity 1: Where to Start

The complexity of youth homelessness can seem overwhelming. Implementing all the strategies we provide in this book at the same time may be difficult for a district or school that is beginning this conversation. Susan Sclafani, former deputy superintendent of Houston (TX) public schools, when asked where to start in reforming a large urban school district with enormous challenges, replied, "Do something" (see Skrla & Scheurich, 2003). Where a school or district starts its work toward improving schooling for children and youth experiencing homelessness is less important than that the organization starts somewhere. Simple awareness might serve. As a participant in Brown's (2016) work put it, "It seem[s] to me that a lot of the people who have the power to make national changes are very unaware of the conditions or the circumstances we live under."

We provided several ideas at the end of each chapter to begin thinking about how to identify and address barriers within the local context. For educators looking for a more holistic way to think about initiating a review of the district and/or school site (both for compliance with federal and state law and toward incorporating a trauma-informed approach to services), we recommend considering the following questions:

- **How do students experience homelessness in your school or district?** This may be more difficult to assess than just looking at numbers of students categorized as homeless in the district databases. Conversations with educators and community leaders may be needed to help judge the accuracy of those numbers and to learn what categories of homelessness the students experience.

- **How does your school or district identify students experiencing homelessness?** This involves a review of the coding system, student registration materials, and training programs for staff and faculty members. In order to begin serving these students, they need to first be accurately identified.
- **How do students experiencing homelessness perform academically?** Many districts and schools do not track academic progress for these students. Informal systems may need to be created. Ideally, districts will require these students' progress to be reported as part of equity reports submitted by school sites.
- **Do policies at school and district levels limit educational access and success for students without residential stability?** This involves a wide range of issues from transportation and registration to enrollment in college access programs and participation in extracurricular activities. As these policies are reviewed, steps need to be taken to adjust any policy that limits education participation. Further, conversations about providing priority access to college access programming should occur, per federal mandates.
- **What partnerships could be built to increase educational access and success for students experiencing homelessness?** The multifaceted nature of this social issue requires a complex approach with wraparound services. These partnerships may involve social service agencies, homeless shelters, postsecondary institutions, counseling services, health care agencies, and family programming. Based upon the specific needs of students in the school or district, educators and administrations should consider what partners may exist in the community that could help support students without residential stability.
- **What would a comprehensive program look like in the local context?** This will depend on the local needs of the students and the resources available.
- **What strategies can be implemented to ensure continued review of policies and practices?** The student needs may evolve over time as economic and social situations change in the local, state, and national context. A thorough review of policies should probably take place every 3 to 5 years.

Activity 2: Developing a Plan of Action

A plan of action, ideally, is a collaborative effort meant to guide a school, state, or district in moving forward in supporting students and families experiencing homelessness. Throughout the book, educators have had the opportunity to identify areas of success as well as issues that could be addressed to improve student experiences and outcomes. We encourage educators to develop a plan to move forward as a school, district, and/or state (Appendix I may also be useful in developing a plan). Creating a manageable and informed plan will be critical to its success and sustainability.

Consider the following:

- What resources or trainings exist or could be developed? How often will they be offered or updated? Are there local or national organizations that provide trainings (e.g., SchoolHouse Connection)?
- What resources (human, capital, etc.) already exist within the school? Are these resources being adequately utilized?
- Who else could be brought into the conversation?
- What community resources exist to supplement or bolster school efforts? How can the school/district develop/strengthen community partnerships?
    - » For example, SchoolHouse Connection (n.d.) recommends hosting a community breakfast with local service providers to learn about programs and resources they provide. This can also be developed into a list of community resources that school staff and families can easily access.
- Who will lead or coordinate these efforts?
- How can educators create caring systems of accountability that allow for continuous learning, reinforcement of McKinney-Vento basics, and problem-solving as challenges or issues arise?
- How will information be shared? (e.g. newsletter, email, bulletin, etc.)
- What will be the schedule for information exchange/sharing of resources/updates? (e.g. quarterly, monthly, etc.).

APPENDIX A

Visualizing Doubled-Up Residences

Purpose: *This activity gives educators an opportunity to explore the experiences of students and families who live doubled-up. While this form of homelessness is the most common for schools and districts, it can be the most difficult to recognize.*

Doubled-up residences can exist in many different formations. We provide two illustrations of different arrangements to help educators visualize what the experience looks like and how it can influence students. We here discuss two residences with family members living together; however, Chapter 3 included an example of non-relatives and a further discussion of how this residential arrangement falls within the classification of homeless. The arrangements vary greatly—the overarching similarity is that families have inadequate space, and the residence is not stable. (For further discussion and examples, see Hallett, 2012a).

Juan lived in an 800-square-foot apartment with his immediate family and extended family representing at least two other households—grandparents and an adult uncle. His mother, aunt, and uncle each worked a minimum-wage job; however, they could not individually afford to rent an apartment independently. In addition, the family needed to care for Juan's grandparents, who could no longer work. Each household needed the financial contribution of the other households, or all the family members would be without a home. Magnifying the instability of this living arrangement, the rental agreement had only his grandparents listed, which meant that the apartment manager could kick all the families out at any time for violating the terms of the contract.

To complicate the situation, the family groups did not want to live together. Each household was willing to take an alternative arrangement if the opportunity emerged. The financial stress as well as interpersonal conflict created constant tension in the home. For example, the families had separate shelves in the refrigerator and arguments erupted when food went missing. And navigating one bathroom for nine people led to frustration—especially in the morning when everyone was trying to get ready.

Juan, a senior in high school, noted that he was the only person who had his own room—he put a mattress in the closet of the bedroom he shared with his mother and younger siblings. He had a small light that enabled him to close the door when he wanted privacy, including when he was doing homework. Each morning, he walked his siblings to school because his mom was already at work. Juan took responsibility for being a role model for his siblings and tried to help them with their homework.

Marco lived in a 1500-square-foot house with his immediate family and his extended family. This arrangement emerged when his immediate family experienced financial crises after his parents' divorce when he was in elementary school. His mom moved out of state, and he never saw her again. His

Figure A.1

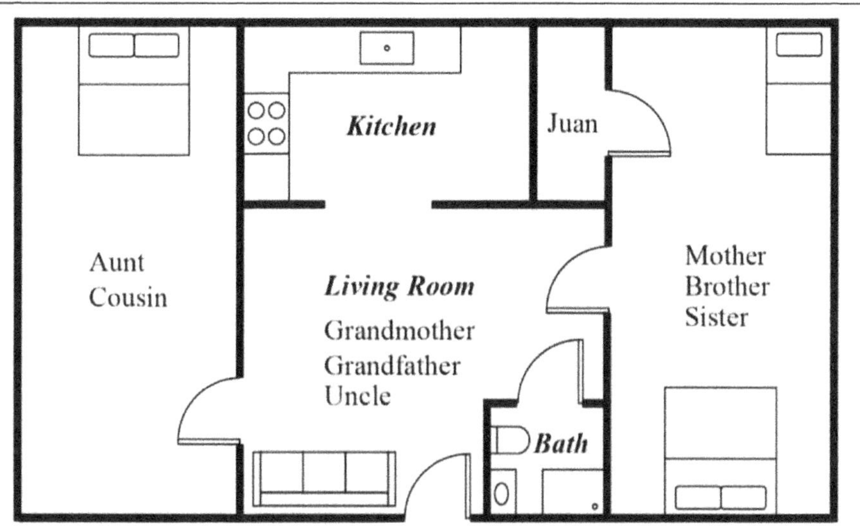

Figure A.2

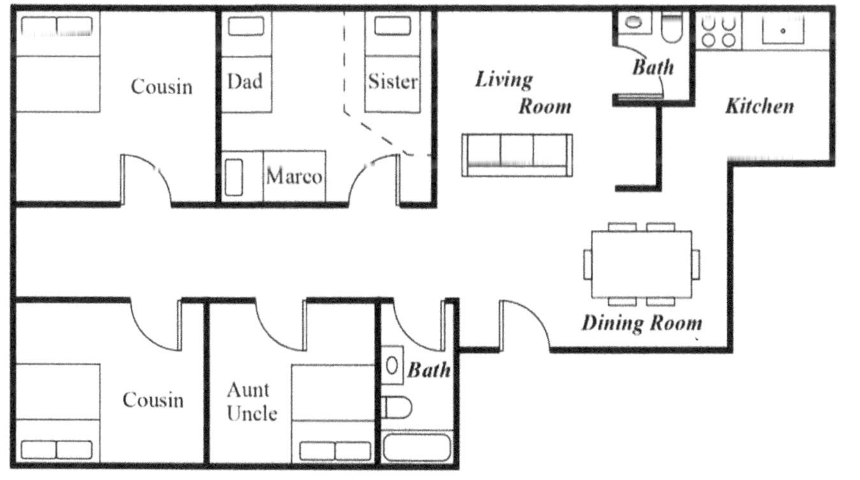

father sought refuge with his sister and her family. Whereas Juan's extended family needed the other members' financial contributions to pay rent and bills, Marco's family relied on his aunt and uncle, but the converse was not true. As such, his immediate family could be kicked out at any time if a disagreement emerged.

Marco (a senior in high school), his dad, and his older sister shared one room at the time we met them—they put a curtain up to give his sister some privacy in the corner of the room. The extended family shared the living room, dining room and kitchen; however, Marco knew it was his aunt's and uncle's home. He got along with his aunt, uncle, and cousins. They shared resources with Marco's family. However, the possibility consistently existed that his family could be kicked out with little or no notice—his aunt and uncle owned the home, and his father had no claim to a right to live there.

APPENDIX B

Student Perspective—Finding Educational Opportunities and Trusting Adults

Contributed by Carlos A. Galan, PhD

Purpose: *This vignette provides educators an opportunity to explore the importance of trusting relationships in education. Carlos lived in a doubled-up residence with three family units living in a small two-bedroom apartment. He speaks about how educational mentors helped him become more fully engaged with school and eventually transition to higher education.*

I was 15 years old when I immigrated from El Salvador to the United States. In El Salvador, I was part of a small and rural community. Everyone knew each other. But in the United States, everything was bigger; this was particularly true for my school. I attended the largest high school in California—so many students crowded the hallways between passing periods that it was nearly impossible to make it to class on time.

To accommodate everyone, the school divided its students into three tracks (A, B, and C) that determined both academic tracking and the timing of when students of each respective track were in the building throughout the year. Depending on the track we were placed in, some decisions about our postsecondary options were made for us. Looking back, I realize how lucky I was to be enrolled in the A track. I had access to the Newcomer Program, where I developed my skills in English as a newly arrived student to the United States. Years later, when it was time to apply to college, being part of the A track allowed me to receive messaging and support to apply for college and financial aid, while my friends in the B and C tracks were not in classes at that time.

The school system was foreign to me and my family. My mother was trying to figure out life in a new country. When she learned that schools provided free meals to students, she agreed to hold me back a year so that we could benefit from the free and reduced lunch program for one more year. Even though I was supposed to start in 10th grade based on my age and previous schooling in El Salvador, I was enrolled as a 9th-grader and placed in the Newcomer

Program. In trying to get a year of free and reduced lunch, my mother bought me additional time to transition to the U.S. school system.

At school, I was shy for a long time. I was a good soccer player, which helped me make friends and meet my soccer coach, Mrs. Carr-Swain. Mrs. Carr-Swain was the first trusting adult I had in school. She always gave me snacks after practice. She believed in me and made me realize the importance of having good grades as a student-athlete. After taking the time to get to know me personally, she learned that I had few opportunities to do homework in my crowded apartment. She introduced me to an after-school program where I could go after soccer practice to complete my homework. In Mrs. Carr-Swain, I found someone who provided support, expressed care, and created spaces where I felt that I could belong—the soccer team and a tutoring program.

I had no long-term plans for my studies beyond keeping good grades to play soccer. However, that changed when I was selected to be part of a college preparation program that included a mentor from a local university. My mentor, Bill, was a professor and one of the first people to talk to me about college. At one point, I thought he was a social worker who had come to take me away from my family because of our crowded living situation. Thankfully, he showed up at my high school to mentor me through the college application process. By guiding me through college applications, Bill expanded my possibilities by encouraging me think about going to college. He helped me get admitted to UCLA as well as guiding me in finding financial aid to cover the costs.

Throughout the years, I never let go of Bill's mentorship. His guidance and friendship have been invaluable in helping me set both short- and long-term goals. As a first-generation student from a working-class background, sometimes it is hard to think beyond the day-to-day—the surviving. However, having someone who has helped me reflect and pause has been instrumental in advancing my academic and professional life. As a first-generation college student, I did not know what I did not know. I understand now that to navigate the school system, we need access to trusting adults who express care for us, challenge us to grow, expand our possibilities, and support us. However, unlike me, many of my peers did not have access to a trusting adult as they navigated schooling and professional life.

When I think about what it takes to support first-generation, working-class students with unstable living situations, I reflect on the difference that having access to a trusting adult can make. In my case, having Mrs. Carr-Swain and Bill made all the difference. As of writing this vignette, I recently completed my doctoral degree and have begun my first year as an assistant professor. My research focuses on increasing educational opportunities for other students.

APPENDIX C

McKinney-Vento and ESSA Summary

Purpose: *This appendix provides a summary of the McKinney-Vento and ESSA policies that guide schools, districts, and states in designing and implementing services and supports for students experiencing homelessness and housing insecurity.*

Policy	McKinney-Vento	ESSA Revisions
Definition of Homeless	Individuals who lack a fixed, regular, and adequate nighttime residence. This definition includes children and youth who are sharing the housing of other persons due to loss of housing, economic hardship, or similar reason (doubled-up); youth living in motels, hotels, trailer parks, and camping groups; those in emergency and transitional shelters; young people abandoned in hospitals; children living in public and private spaces not typically used as housing for humans; youth residing in cars, parks, abandoned buildings, and train stations or similar settings; foster youth awaiting placement; and migratory children who fit within the above housing situations.	Foster children and youth awaiting placement were removed from the definition of homeless. ESSA requires state Title I plans to ensure collaboration with the state child welfare agency to ensure educational stability of children and youth in foster care.

(*Continued*)

Policy	McKinney-Vento	ESSA Revisions
Segregation	No state receiving McKinney-Vento funding shall segregate youth experiencing homelessness into separate schools or programs, with the rare exception of a few schools functioning prior to 2000.	No changes under ESSA—this requirement remains in place.
School of Origin	Students can remain at school of origin throughout their homeless experiences. If students become residentially stabilized, they can remain at school of origin until the end of the academic term. School districts must provide transportation to school of origin if the family is beyond walking distance to school.	School of origin explicitly includes the feeder schools at all levels of education, including preschool. If the district determines that school of origin is not in the best interest of the student, a written explanation must be provided to the parents, guardian, or youth (if unaccompanied). This document must be written in a way that is accessible to the intended reader. Parents and guardians get to decide about remaining at school of origin and have the right to appeal school decisions that are counter to their desire to have their student remain at the school of origin.
Policy Review	States, districts, and school sites must review all policies to ensure that youth in homeless situations are not denied access to school.	No changes under ESSA.
Homeless Liaison	Every school district must identify a homeless liaison.	The homeless liaison must receive professional development in order to carry out their duties.

Policy	McKinney-Vento	ESSA Revisions
State Coordinator	The state must gather information about the nature and extent of problems related to youth experiencing homelessness gaining access to public schools; identify special needs of this subpopulation; and report on district processes related to access and identification processes.	States must post the number of youth experiencing homelessness on the state website; identify educational barriers for these youth; provide professional development for district liaisons; and respond to inquiries from parents and youth related to these provisions.
Enrollment	Youth experiencing homelessness can enroll immediately, whether or not they have health and immunization records, transcripts, or proof of residency; can meet dress code requirements; or have other paperwork related to enrollment. Unaccompanied youth can enroll without a parent or guardian.	Outstanding fees or fines and excessive absences cannot be used to delay enrollment. Application and enrollment deadlines cannot be used to deny access to school for this subpopulation.
Funding		ESSA clarifies that subgrant funds can be used to attract, engage, and retain homeless children and youth who are not enrolled in school and can be used for extraordinary or emergency assistance to enable homeless youth to attend school. It also provides more flexibility in how Title I funds can be used to serve homeless students
Access to Activities		Clarifies that states must have procedures to ensure that homeless children and youth do not face barriers to accessing academic and extracurricular activities.

(*Continued*)

Policy	McKinney-Vento	ESSA Revisions
Credit		States are required to develop procedures to identify and remove barriers that prevent students from receiving appropriate credit for full or partial coursework satisfactorily completed while attending a prior school.
FERPA		A homeless student's living arrangement must be treated as an education record, subject to all the protections of FERPA.
Special Education	The law covers students from birth to age 22 for PK–12 education purposes. Extending the age allows for support for students with special needs who may be working on transition plans.	The school district shall coordinate special education services within the LEA, and with other involved LEAs.
College Access and Career Counseling		Homeless liaisons must inform unaccompanied youth of their rights and independent status in relation to FAFSA.

APPENDIX D

Guidance for New Homeless Education State Coordinators

Contributed by Ruth Uhey, EdD, Education Associate, Out-of-School Time Programs and Students Experiencing Homelessness & Delaware McKinney-Vento State Coordinator

Purpose: *This appendix provides guidance for new homeless education state coordinators. In particular, a current state coordinator offers advice about the key tasks and goals that new coordinators should consider as they transition into this role.*

Dear New State Coordinator:

On August 1, 2022, I was honored to step into the role of the McKinney-Vento State Coordinator for Delaware. At that point in time, I had served Delaware public education for 21 years, and specifically on the state level for 18 of those years. As a new State Coordinator, I relied on my educational and professional backgrounds, known resources, and well-established relationships, as well as my own personal experiences of homelessness. Although I was confident to begin strong, I questioned myself: *What don't I know?* I reflected on what it was like being a student experiencing homelessness prior to and after the McKinney-Vento Act becoming law. I also considered societal, political, cultural, and other trends and important issues both locally and globally. I thought about what today's student might be experiencing, and their potential needs. Then I considered the role of the local education agency liaison, the information that they might need for determining eligibility, providing resources, and the geographical differences throughout the state to meet needs. Additionally, I thought about students moving across borders from neighboring states and beyond, the partnerships I would need to put in place, and the importance of staying current.

As a new state coordinator, the challenges and needs of students and families experiencing homelessness can be overwhelming if you do not know where to begin. Therefore, start with the McKinney-Vento Act, as it establishes the state coordinator position and identifies seven functions. Each function is an important link connecting the federal mandates with state and local (district/

charter/site) operations to ensure that students experiencing homelessness have immediate access to a free, appropriate public education and are in compliance with federal regulations (42 U.S.C. § 11432 (f)(1)). Learn the Act's definition of homelessness, as it differs from other federal agencies', and the seven required functions. Also, establishing resources and relationships is critical for success, as your role requires the ability to partner with federal, state, and local government agencies as well as community and faith-based organizations to meet specific needs and to remove educational barriers. The federal, state, and local levels have three common and essential elements, which include 1) requirements and expectations, 2) priorities (immediate, short- and long-term), and 3) supports available to assist in fulfilling their duties. Listed below are a few important areas and resources for each level:

- Federal level—
  - » Your federal contact at OESE (Office of Elementary and Secondary Education at the U.S. Department of Education)
  - » Federal nonregulatory guidance
  - » Federal funding and current grants
  - » Data reporting requirements and deadlines
  - » Compliance monitoring requirements
  - » State coordinator meeting dates
  - » Other state coordinators
  - » National Center for Homeless Education (NCHE)
  - » National Association for the Education of Homeless Children and Youth (NAEHCY)
  - » SchoolHouse Connection
- State level—
  - » Your state plan
  - » Your state's policies and procedures (attendance, dispute resolution, etc.)
  - » Existing grants
  - » Data reporting requirements and deadlines
  - » Access to your student database system
  - » Statewide community partners
- Local district/charter/site level—
  - » The federal law establishes ten duties for the local education agency liaison (42 U.S.C.§ 11432 (g)(6)(A)). A new State Coordinator needs to know who the local liaisons are; their needs, such as training and professional development; and their existing policies and practices.

With each new school year, I keep in mind my original question, *What don't I know?*, to stay focused on current trends, to think outside the box regarding potential needs, to help others, and to seek resources for myself and for Delaware's statewide liaisons. As you step into your new role, you and the work that you do are important, and essential for students and families experiencing homelessness. There are many of us who started where you are now. We want you to feel encouraged, and know that there are people, your new partners, who are willing to help.

QUESTIONS FOR DISCUSSION

1. What knowledge do you currently have about the local education agencies in your state? Do you know who the school's Education for Homeless Children and Youth (EHCY) Program liaisons are? Do you know which school districts or charters have McKinney-Vento subgrants? Do you know or have access to their subgrant amounts or Title I Set-Aside funding amounts and the allowable uses?
2. How might different community organizations partner together to meet the needs of students and families experiencing homelessness? What would a successful partnership look like?
3. Do you know your state's homeless data? Do you have access to this information? Have you read or have access to your state plan? If not, whom could you contact for assistance?
4. Do you know who your federal Office of Elementary and Secondary Education (OESE) contact is? Are you familiar with the National Center for Homeless Education (NCHE) or the National Association for the Education of Homeless Children and Youth (NAEHCY)?

APPENDIX E

Family Navigating Housing Instability

Contributed by April Anderson, District Liaison for Special Populations, Red Clay Consolidated School District, Wilmington, Delaware

Purpose: *This vignette provides educators an opportunity for educators to reflect on the challenges of supporting a family who is highly mobile. The family's experience requires reflecting on school of origin, transportation, and peer and teacher relationships. Educators are encouraged to consider how districts, county offices, and community groups could be part of the process.*

The Johnsons are a family of seven individuals—a single mom and six children ages 5–17. All of the children are enrolled in the Red Rock School District. Ms. Johnson lost her job in May. By August, she is 3 months behind in rent. As the school year begins, the family is facing eviction. She needs to design a housing plan for her family. The decision is made to divide the siblings between a grandparent's home and a local motel with mom. Eva (15), Adam (17), and Olivia (13) live with their grandmother. Lily (5), Jordan (7), and Journee (10) stay at the Best Nights Inn with mom.

Pause to reflect:

- Are the three siblings living with their mother in a hotel eligible for McKinney-Vento protections and support?
- Are the three siblings living with their grandmother in her home eligible for McKinney-Vento protections and support?
- Is there additional information you would need to determine their eligibility and enroll the students in the school?
- Are the students eligible to remain at the school across town where they attended before losing housing?
- If some or all the children are eligible for McKinney-Vento protections and support, what could be a best practice to ensure that services are in place at the start of the school year?
- What are needed services beyond school that would support family needs and student learning?

- What people and organizations in the community might be of assistance in meeting the "non-school" needs identified?

After the three older kids have lived with their grandmother for a month, the landlord serves an eviction notice. The lease she had signed stated that the legal capacity limit of her two-bedroom apartment was three people. The grandmother lives on a fixed income and has no choice but to have her grandchildren move in hopes of negotiating with landlord to cancel the eviction. Eva, Adam, and Olivia transition to their aunt's home in the next county, about a 45-minute drive from their current schools.

Pause to reflect:

- Can and should the siblings continue attending their school of origin? Why?
- If the students remain at school of origin, are the children entitled to transportation to and from their school of origin?
- Two of the children were in after-school sports and the other participated in a college preparation program before school. Are the students eligible for transportation to these activities that are outside of school hours? If so, how could that work? If not, how do you share this information with the students?

Over winter break, Ms. Johnson finds a job two counties south of their original home—about an hour away from their current schools. The entire family moves into a motel in the area. Mom's plan is to live in the motel until she can secure more permanent housing near her new job, which appears to be stable employment at this point.

Pause to reflect:

- Should the older siblings enroll in the school district in the attendance zone of the motel or remain enrolled in their school of origin? What about the younger siblings? Why or why not? What questions and conversations will best guide your decision?
- How can the students be supported in enrolling in the public attendance zone school if that decision is in their best interest?
- What would the transportation plan look like if the students remain in their school of origin for the remainder of the academic year? What would it look like if they remain at their school of origin for the remainder of their academic careers?
- What strategies would you use to determine their best interests?
- What are needed services beyond school that would support family needs and student learning?
- What people and organizations in the community might be of assistance in meeting the non-school needs identified?

APPENDIX F

Transportation To and From School of Origin

Contributed by Lori Knochelmann,
McKinney-Vento Coordinator,
Covington Independent Public Schools, Covington, KY

Purpose: *This activity gives educators an opportunity to reflect on the challenges and opportunities related to providing transportation for students experiencing homelessness and residential mobility.*

The McKinney-Vento Act requires school, districts and states to: (a) review and revise policies to remove barriers to students' identification as homeless, school enrollment, and attendance; and (b) provide transportation for eligible students to public schools—including school of origin. Many schools and districts find providing transportation particularly challenging when these students move outside of the school's attendance boundary.

School of origin is the school where the student attended when they experienced homelessness. Students can remain enrolled at the school of origin until the end of the school year after the student obtains permanent housing, which means they no longer qualify for accommodations under McKinney-Vento. Parents, guardians, or a liaison for a student experiencing homelessness must be provided information about the student's rights under McKinney-Vento before they make a decision about remaining at school of origin or transferring to the school near their new residential location.

The homeless coordinator for the district must:

- Cover the cost or collaborate with a partner to cover the costs—parents, students, or guardians should not be expected to pay for transportation.
- Provide transportation that is comparable to that of other students.
- Begin transportation promptly after identification to prevent disruptions to attendance.

- Include transportation for extracurricular activities.
- If a parent disputes a district's decision not to transport a student, the district should continue to provide transportation until the dispute is resolved.
- Coordinators *must* train staff each year on the rights and needs of homeless students, as well as the need for sensitivity and confidentiality when referring students to a homeless coordinator. Training includes encouraging educators to create trusting relationships with students and families so they can become aware of transportation issues. This training also includes bus drivers and others who work in transportation—they play an important role in supporting students and identifying when issues emerge related to transportation.

Transportation across district boundaries can be challenging. A few things to consider:

- If it is in the student's best interest to attend a school of origin in another district, transportation must be provided for the student to that school.
- Depending upon the location of the school district, the school of origin may involve considering transportation for students who move to an adjacent district in another state. (The federal policy does not explicitly say whether students who cross state lines are exempt from this mandate.)
- Transportation involves financial costs and staff time to coordinate. When students cross district boundaries, both districts—the school of origin and the location where the family resides—have a shared responsibility. The districts should develop a plan, which could include:
    - » One district coordinates transportation and then both split the cost, which may involve one district sending an invoice to the other each month.
    - » One district covers the cost of transportation to school and the other covers the cost of transportation from school.
    - » Districts split the costs and coordination by fall and spring semester.
    - » Districts close to each other likely have more than one student moving between boundaries. The districts could divide students to share cost and responsibility.
    - » Districts should have a mutually agreed-upon plan to avoid sending an invoice at the end of the academic year to another district without advance knowledge.

Covering the cost of transportation:

- Most states provide McKinney-Vento subgrant funds, which require districts to apply. These funds can be used to defray the cost of transportation to the school of origin.
- A portion of Title I, Part A of the Elementary and Secondary Education Act of 1965 must be set aside to support students experiencing homelessness. The funds can be used to cover the excess cost of transportation to the school of origin [20 U.S.C. §6313(c)(3)(C)(ii)].
- Districts may also look at current transportation patterns to see if minor shifts could be made at no or minimum cost. For example, a student could walk to the school closest to their residence and get on a school bus that drops them off at their school of origin.

Methods of transportation:

- Students can walk to school or a pickup location, if within a mile or whatever the standard district/school policy is
- Yellow bus through your transportation department
- Contracted 1099 SUV drivers (include cameras, signage, training, and background check)
- EverDriven (expensive, but full service and track students)
- Business Uber
- Cab or taxi services
- Public transportation passes (some cities have free or reduced-cost passes for students)
- Gas cards (some companies have "fuel only" cards to reduce concern about purchasing other things)
- Mileage reimbursement for family
- Volunteers (be cautious about liability issues and require background check)
- Ideas to save money:
    - » Consider ways to prevent fraud, waste, and abuse like a gas calculator or contract.
    - » Brainstorm cost-saving measures with other stakeholders
    - » LEAs make the final decision on the mode of transportation

APPENDIX G

School Community Mapping for Students Experiencing Housing Instability

Purpose: *This activity provides educators a structured way to create a community map of the resources available in the local context. (This could be used to look at the state or district context as well.) Educators will explore the multiple individuals, groups or agencies that could become partners in supporting students and families experiencing homelessness. The diagram below serves as a starting point; however, there may be other groups or people in your community that are not listed in the examples below. The activity was adapted from Duncan (2016).*

Figure G.1. Asset-Mapping Template for Schools and Districts

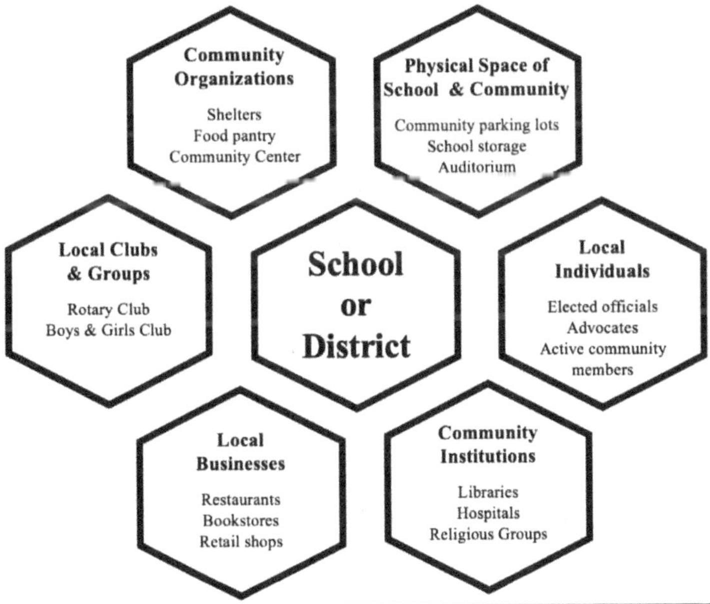

Community Organizations
Shelters
Food pantry
Community Center

Physical Space of School & Community
Community parking lots
School storage
Auditorium

Local Clubs & Groups
Rotary Club
Boys & Girls Club

School or District

Local Individuals
Elected officials
Advocates
Active community members

Local Businesses
Restaurants
Bookstores
Retail shops

Community Institutions
Libraries
Hospitals
Religious Groups

Please keep in mind that this should, if possible, be a collaborative effort among a team of school and community leaders. The primary objective is to identify the strengths of the community and find ways that partnerships can be cultivated and leveraged to support the needs of students and families experiencing housing instability.

Start with your school—What are the assets of the school that can be harnessed? What are the current assets of the school community that are already in place/working to support unstably housed students (e.g., McKinney-Vento implementation, school liaison, after-school programming, etc.)?

Surveying the physical space and its resources—Consider the school layout and the surrounding community. (e.g., storage space, bulletin boards, meeting rooms, parking lots, etc.). This information can be useful when considering how best to disseminate school supplies, transportation funds, etc. to students in a private, discreet, and dignified manner. It could also be used to identify school space for local organizations, nonprofits, or businesses to use when providing resources and support—for example, a local dentist who is willing to provide free dental checkups to students at the school.

Local nonprofits/community organizations—What organizations already provide support to low-income and/or unhoused individuals and families, such as a food pantry, overnight shelter, transportation vouchers, etc. Knowing who they are, what they provide, and where they are located can result in the development of a list of resources that can be shared with students and families.

Local groups/clubs—Does your community have a local Boys and Girls Club, Rotary Club, etc., interested in partnering with the school to provide resources/support in the form of human capital (volunteers) or financial capital that could supplement McKinney-Vento funds (e.g. funds for field trips, prom, and other school-related activities not covered under McKinney-Vento)?

Local individuals—What are the skills and strengths of local residents not affiliated with particular groups or organizations, but who have a demonstrated commitment to their local community and strong ties to other locals? Who are the local city council representatives?

Local businesses—What businesses or business organizations (Chamber of Commerce, merchants, etc.) exist in the community? How might their capital and resources be leveraged to support students? Are there opportunities to develop collaborations for student employment, internships, and so on?

Community institutions—What are the local institutions such as libraries, churches, hospitals, museums, social service agencies, block clubs, and the like? Developing partnerships and collaborations with these institutions can support the needs of students and families, for example referrals for health needs, or even a designated study space at the local library. Community connections also allow for referrals that serve to strengthen the whole family, which ultimately benefits students.

The idea is to document the many local assets of the community, to create a sort of "inventory" that can be referred to as your school team/PLC works to develop or strengthen the support provided to students and families who are housing-unstable. We understand that schools alone cannot provide for the many out-of-school needs of students and families; therefore, creating partnerships through mutually beneficial relationships can help to fill the gaps in service as well as alleviate some of the pressure placed on schools and school personnel. Over time, the goal is to create an ecosystem of support and coordination in which the school is well-integrated into its local community. It also allows the local community to get to know school personnel, students, and families, ideally creating a stronger and safer community for all.

Considerations:

1. Where are the local social service agencies providing housing services? Are there programs and/or individuals the school can collaborate with to support student stability and academic access/success?
2. Where is the local food pantry? Social security office? Health and human services? Are there programs families and students can be referred to for assistance—in particular to meet needs that are beyond the capacity of the school to provide, but that impact student learning, behavior, and academic outcomes?
3. Is there a school event that would be a good opportunity to collaborate with local organizations to connect parents to local resources (e.g., teacher-parent conferences, school plays, etc.)? Keep in mind that this does not need to be a big event or production. The goal is to slowly and strategically build partnerships over time that can better support the needs of students, families, and their respective communities.

APPENDIX H

Participatory Action Research

Purpose: *This appendix provides an overview of participant action research, which is a tool that educators can use to explore issues of concern within their local context. In addition to summarizing the concept, we provide advice about how to leverage this tool to gather information needed to improve the services and supports offered by a school, district, or state.*

Participatory Action Research (PAR) (Payne, 2017) allows researchers to meaningfully and deliberately partner with community members most impacted by housing instability. PAR was developed as a bottom-up approach to understanding community issues such as crime, education, and health care (Payne, 2017). PAR aims to build capacity among all research team members, to uncover short- and long-term solutions to difficult social problems. Importantly, PAR includes members of those under study as part of the research team to build in mechanisms of accountability to yield a more fair and guided analysis of the data.

PAR encompasses many forms of participatory work, including but not limited to Youth Participatory Action Research (YPAR) and Community-Based Participatory Research (CBPR). YPAR "promotes youth's involvement in their communities and the development of leadership skills. It emphasizes the development of young people's knowledge, skills, and abilities to be experts on issues of importance to them and catalyze systemic change in collaboration with their peers and supportive adults" (Powers & Allaman, 2013, p. 2) and has been found useful when working to center youth voice and perspectives into community and research work (Aviles & Grigalunas, 2018). Community-based participatory research (CBPR) refers to "research activities carried out in local settings in which community members actively collaborate with professionally trained researchers. CBPR is not linked to a particular academic field, but is instead utilized in a range of disciplines, particularly in the health and social sciences, community development, the humanities, and regional planning" (Duke, 2020, p. 2). Key principles of CBPR include:

- recognizing community as a unit of identity;
- drawing from community strengths and resources;
- facilitating equitable partnerships and power-sharing arrangements;

- promoting co-learning and capacity-building among all partners;
- achieving a mutually beneficial balance between research and action;
- developing and maintaining partnerships through a cyclical and iterative process;
- involving all partners in project dissemination; and
- sharing a long-term commitment to partnership sustainability.

Given the youth population of students experiencing housing instability and the impact on communities, these two forms of PAR are most appropriate for engaging youth and families facing housing instability. Once again, these approaches challenge notions of deficit among students and families experiencing housing instability. Instead, we focus on the assets, talents, knowledge, and capacity of people impacted by housing challenges. Focusing on the resilience and strengths of McKinney-Vento students and families resists characterizations that perpetuate paternalism, sympathy, and charity, resulting in collaborative and mutually beneficial approaches to McKinney-Vento implementation within and outside of school settings. For those interested in taking these relationships a step further, we recommend also partnering with local colleges and universities to develop outcome measures that can be used to document the effectiveness of school–community partnerships in serving the academic, subsistence, and well-being needs of students and families experiencing housing instability.

EXAMPLE OF YPAR

The following example draws from Johnson et al. (2017), *"I Learned That We Matter": Reflections on Strategies to Engage Formerly Homeless Young Adults in Youth Participatory Action Research*. This project leveraged photos as a data gathering tool, but many other approaches to data-gathering could be used. We highlight this example to inspire conversations about if/how to empower students to explore experiences of homelessness in the local context and provide recommendations related to improving support.

Growing evidence affirms the benefits of Youth Participatory Action Research (YPAR), a youth-centered form of community-based participatory research that aims to empower youth in schools and community-based settings. The Young Adult Photovoice Project (YAPP) was a YPAR study designed to assess, document, and disseminate an understanding of the barriers to obtaining adequate nutrition faced by formerly homeless young adults living in permanent supportive housing in San Francisco. Nine young adult residents between the ages of 18 and 25 participated. Study participants were given digital cameras and received training in photography as well as in the safety and ethics of taking pictures. Each week participants chose a prompt to guide their photo taking and participated in critical reflection and dialogue around their photos. Participants subsequently created captions and wrote narratives for their photographs. The project culminated in a photography exhibit in downtown San Francisco, with media coverage.

Benefits from YAPP participation included: increased ability/comfort with group work; increased self-confidence in creative expression and public speaking; improved photography skills; improved ability to give and receive constructive criticism; increased perceived self-efficacy in completing a project from start to finish; and an increased sense of self-worth. Study strategies that facilitated participant engagement included: being flexible and making provisions to accommodate participant schedules; framing the project as an "internship" and paying hourly wages; providing skill-building components in photography and constructive criticism; providing an opportunity for participants to present their work in a public exhibit; and deferring to participants' own definitions of study issues. Challenges to participant engagement included: interpersonal conflict among group members; competing priorities in participant's lives such as jobs and child care; participants' mental and physical health; aversions to group work due to social anxiety and trauma; the tension of balancing project rules with accommodations for participants' needs; and insufficient participant training concerning how to interact with the media.

District/School Professional Development on Students Experiencing Homelessness—Review and Resources

Purpose: *The chart below could be used to assess and evaluate school or district professional development activities related to students and families who experience homelessness. It is adapted from materials produced by the Indiana Department of Education. It could be used by a variety of individuals and groups, including school leaders, school/district planning teams, and PLCs.*

Prompt	Yes, No, Unsure, N/A	Challenges	School, District, State Supports	Community Supports	Action Plan
Prompt 1: Does the school district have a policy that requires ongoing (at minimum annual) training on the special issues and needs of children and youth without homes for all professional and classified staff who interact with these children and youth including:					
(a) teachers, aides, student teachers, tutors, and other instructional personnel? (b) principals and other administrative personnel? (c) counselors, nurses, librarians, diagnosticians, social workers, therapists, and other professional support personnel? (d) cafeteria workers, bus drivers, custodians, secretaries, clerks, crossing guards, and other classified staff?					
Prompt 2: Does the school district have a written policy or procedure that identifies the person(s) responsible for ensuring that all school personnel have staff development oriented toward the needs of children and youth in homeless situations? Have all school board members and school personnel, including all professional and classified staff who interact with children, been provided with staff development (minimum 2 hours) that includes:					
(a) definition of homelessness? (b) causes of homelessness? (c) barriers to enrollment confronting children and youth experiencing homelessness? (d) barriers to school success confronting children and youth experiencing homelessness? (e) requirements of the [McKinney-Vento and ESSA] related to children and youth without homes?					

(f) strategies through which schools can help students in homeless situations achieve success? (g) emotional impact of inappropriate or thoughtless comments or actions that focus on the child's homelessness as a way of singling out, ignoring, teasing, or disciplining a child? (h) potentially life-threatening consequences of revealing information about children from battered families? (i) community resources and services available to students without homes? (j) strategies for helping parents and students become aware of and sensitive to issues confronting students experiencing homelessness?					
Prompt 3: Do school personnel have access to materials (brochures, articles, books, curriculum materials, video presentations, etc.) that can assist personnel, parents, or students in understanding the causes of homelessness, the needs of children and youth experiencing homelessness, and the ways in which public schools can better respond to those needs?					

(*Continued*)

Prompt	Yes, No, Unsure, N/A	Challenges	School, District, State Supports	Community Supports	Action Plan
Prompt 4: Do school personnel (particularly campus administrators, professional support personnel, and teachers) utilize available materials in assisting other personnel, parents, and students in understanding the causes of homelessness, the needs of children and youth experiencing homelessness, and the ways in which public schools can better respond to those needs?					
Prompt 5: Once school personnel have received training, are efforts made to reduce staff turnover and maintain trained personnel in schools serving shelter populations?					

Adapted from Indiana Department of Education, 2011, n.p.

References

Advocates for Children of New York. (2024, November 18). *Student homelessness in New York City, 2023–24.* https://advocatesforchildren.org/policy-resource/student-homelessness-data-2024/

Allensworth, E., Ponisciak, S., & Mazzeo, C. (2009). *The schools teachers leave: Teacher mobility in Chicago Public Schools.* Consortium on Chicago School Research, University of Chicago. https://consortium.uchicago.edu/sites/default/files/2018-10/CCSR_Teacher_Mobility.pdf

American Institutes for Research. (2014). *America's youngest outcasts: A report card on child homelessness.* Author.

Aviles, A. M., & Grigalunas (2018). "Project awareness": Fostering social justice youth development to counter youth experiences of housing instability, trauma and injustice. *Children and Youth Services Review, 84,* 229–238. http://dx.doi.org/10.1016/j.childyouth.2017.12.013

Aviles de Bradley, A. M. (2015). *From charity to equity—Race, homelessness, and urban schools.* Teachers College Press.

Baggerly, J., & Borkowski, T. (2004). Applying the ASCA national model to elementary school students who are homeless: A case study. *Professional School Counseling, 8*(2), 116–123.

Bassuk, E. L., DeCandia, C. J., Beach, C. A., & Berman, F. (2014). *America's youngest outcasts: A report card on child homelessness.* American Institutes for Research. https://www.air.org/sites/default/files/downloads/report/Americas-Youngest-Outcasts-Child-Homelessness-Nov2014.pdf

Battarai, A. (2024, July 29). More of America's homeless are clocking into jobs each day. *The Washington Post.* https://www.washingtonpost.com/business/2024/07/28/homeless-lack-of-affordable-housing-economy/

Benson, C. (2023). *Child poverty rate still higher than for older populations but declining.* United States Census Bureau. https://www.census.gov/library/stories/2023/12/poverty-rate-varies-by-age-groups.html

Bettencourt, G. M., Irwin, L. N., Todorova, R., Hallett, R. E., & Corwin, Z. B. (2023). The possibilities and precautions of using the designation "at-promise" in higher education research. *Journal of Postsecondary Student Success, 2*(2), 16–29. https://doi.org/10.33009/fsop_jpss132261

Blank, M. J., Jacobson, R., & Melaville, A. (2012). *Achieving results through community school partnerships.* Center for American Progress. https://cdn.americanprogress.org/wp-content/uploads/issues/2012/01/pdf/community_schools.pdf

Brown, E. (2016, June 17). These are the faces of America's growing youth homeless population. *The Washington Post.* Retrieved from https://www.washingtonpost.com/news/education/wp/2016/06/17/these-are-the-faces-of-americas-growing-youth-homeless-population/?hpid=hp_hp-more-top-stories_youthhomeless_130pm%3Ahomepage%2Fstory

Brumley, B., Fantuzzo, J., Perlman, S., & Zager, M. L. (2015). The unique relations between early homeless and educational well-being: An empirical test of the continuum of risk hypothesis. *Child and Youth Services Review, 48,* 31–37.

Calderón, M., Slavin, R., & Sánchez, M. (2011). Effective instruction for English learners. *The Future of Children, 21*(1), 103–127.

Canfield, J. P., Nolan, J., Harley, D., Hardy, A., & Elliott, W. (2015). Using a person-centered approach to examine the impact of homelessness on school absences. *Child and Adolescence Social Work Journal, 33*(3), 199–205.

Castleman, B. L., & Page, L. C. (2013). A trickle or a torrent? Understanding the extent of summer "melt" among college-intending high school graduates. *Social Science Quarterly, 95*(1), 202–220.

Cutuli, J. J., Desjardins, C. D., Herbers, J. E., Long, J. D., Heistad, D., Chan, C., Hinz, E., & Masten, A. S. (2013). Academic achievement trajectories of homeless and highly mobile students: Resilience in the context of chronic and acute risk. *Child Development, 84*(3), 1–28.

Cutuli, J. J., Torres Suarez, S., Truchil, A., Yost, T., & Flack-Green, C. (2024). Strategies to better identify student homelessness using data in an urban school district. *Educational Researcher, 53*(3), 146–155. https://doi.org/10.3102/0013189X231215347

Desimone, L. M., & Long, D. (2010). Teacher effects and the achievement gap: Do teacher and teaching quality influence the achievement gap between black and white and high- and low-SES students in the early grades? *Teachers College Record, 112* (12), 3024–3073.

Desmond, M. (2017). *Evicted: Poverty and profit in the American city.* Crown Publishing.

Desmond, M. (2023). *Poverty, by America.* Crown Publishing.

Dougherty, C. (February 6, 2021). Pandemic's toll on housing: Falling behind, doubling up. *The New York Times.* https://www.nytimes.com/2021/02/06/business/economy/housing-insecurity.html

Duke, M. (2020, November 19). Community-based participatory research. *Oxford Research Encyclopedia of Anthropology.* https://oxfordre.com/anthropology/view/10.1093/acrefore/9780190854584.001.0001/acrefore-9780190854584-e-225.

Duncan, D. (2016). *Asset based community development: Asset mapping toolkit.* Clear Impact. https://clearimpact.com/resources/publications/asset-mapping-toolkit/

Dworsky, A., (2008). *Educating homeless children in Chicago: A case study of children in the family regeneration program.* Chapin Hall at the University of Chicago.

Endres, C., & Cidade, M. (2015). *Federal data summary school years 2011–12 to 2013–2014: Education for homeless children and youth*. National Center for Homeless Education. https://nche.ed.gov/wp-content/uploads/2018/12/data-comp-1112-1314.pdf

Fabino, A. (2024, April 6). Thousands remain homeless 8 months after Maui fire. *Newsweek*. https://www.newsweek.com/maui-wildfire-recovery-housing-challenge-governor-green-update-1886035

Fantuzzo, J. W., LeBoeuf, W. A., Chen, C., Rouse, H. L., & Culhane, D. P. (2012). The unique and combined effects of homelessness and school mobility on the educational outcomes of young children. *Educational Researcher, 41*, 393–402. doi:10.3102/0013189X 12468210

Freeman, L., & Hamilton, D. (2008). *A count of homeless youth in New York City*. Empire State Coalition of Youth and Family Services.

Garet, M. S., Porter, A. C., Desimone, L., Birman, B. F., & Yoon, K S. (2001). What makes professional development effective? Results from a national sample of teachers. *American Educational Research Journal, 38*(4), 915–945.

Goodman, L. S., & Mayer, C. (2018). Homeownership and the American dream. *Journal of Economic Perspectives, 32*(1), 31–52. https://doi.org/10.1257/jep.32.1.31

Government Accountability Office. (2014). *Education of homeless students: Improved program oversight needed*. Author. https://www.gao.gov/products/gao-14-465

Greenhut, S. (2015, Nov. 22). Job rate is up, but so is economic distress in many California cities. *The San Diego Union-Tribune*, A4.

Guinan, B., & Lafortune, J. (2024, March 13). *Learning recovery for homeless students lags behind other high needs groups*. Public Policy Institute of California. https://www.ppic.org/blog/learning-recovery-for-homeless-students-lags-behind-other-high-need-groups/

Hallett, R. E. (2010). Homeless: How residential instability complicates students' lives. *About Campus, 15*(3), 11–16.

Hallett, R. E. (2012a). *Educational experiences of hidden homeless teenagers: Living doubled-up*. Routledge.

Hallett, R. E. (2012b). Living doubled-up: Diverse environments and educational outcomes. *Education & Urban Society, 44*(4), 371–391.

Hallett, R. E., & Crutchfield, R. (2017). *Homelessness and housing insecurity in higher education: A trauma-informed approach to research, policy, and practice*. ASHE Higher Education Report Series. Jossey-Bass.

Hallett, R. E., Crutchfield, R., & Maguire, J. J. (2019). *Addressing homelessness and housing insecurity in higher education: Strategies for educational leaders*. Teachers College Press.

Hallett, R. E., & Freas, A. (2018). Community college students' experiences with homelessness and housing insecurity. *Community College Journal of Research and Practice, 42*(10), 724–739. https://doi.org/10.1080/10668926.2017.1356764

Hallett, R. E., Freas, A., & Mo, E. (2018). The case for a single point of contact for college students experiencing homelessness. *New Directions for Community Colleges, 184*, 39–49. http://dx.doi.org/10.1002/cc.20326

Hallett, R. E., Hypolite, L., Corwin, Z. B., Nagbe, M., & Kezar, A. (2024). *Considering college students as "at-promise"* [Brief]. Pullias Center for Higher Education, University of Southern California.

Hallett, R. E., Kezar, A., Kitchen, J. A., & Perez, R. J. (2023). *Creating a campus-wide culture of student success: An evidence-based approach to supporting low-income, racially minoritized, and first-generation college students.* Taylor & Francis.

Hallett, R. E., Low, J. A., & Skrla, L. (2015a). Beyond backpacks and bus passes: Next steps for a district homeless student initiative. *International Journal of Qualitative Studies in Education, 28*(6), 693–713.

Hallett, R. E., & Skrla, L. (2021). Supporting students who are experiencing homelessness: A brief guide for teachers and schools. *American Educator, 45*(1), 4–9.

Hallett, R. E., Skrla, L., & Low, J. A. (2015b). That is not what homeless is: A school district's journey toward serving homeless, doubled-up, and economically displaced children and youth. *International Journal of Qualitative Studies in Education, 28*(6), 671–692.

Hallett, R. E., & Woelki, W. T. (2025). *Empowering students through college transition plans: Increasing access to postsecondary degree, credential and certificate programs.* Pullias Center for Higher Education at the University of Southern California. https://pullias.usc.edu/download/empowering-students-through-college-transition-plans-increasing-access-to-postsecondary-degree-credential-and-certificate-programs/

Havlik, S. A. (2024). *A single-point-of-contact resource: For professionals who support housing-insecure college-bound youth and postsecondary students* (2nd ed.). National Association for the Education of Homeless Children and Youth. https://naehcy.org/wp-content/uploads/2024/06/NAEHCY_SPOCUserGuideFINAL_v2.pdf

Havlik, S., & Bryan, J. (2015). Addressing the needs of students experiencing homelessness: School counselor preparation. *The Professional Counselor, 5*(2), 200–216.

Health Care for the Homeless Clinicians' Network. (2010). Delivering trauma-informed services. *Healing Hands, 14*(6), 1–8. https://nhchc.org/wp-content/uploads/2019/08/DecHealingHandsWeb.pdf

Heerde, J. A., Pallotta-Chiarolli, M., & Parolini, A. (2020). "I dropped out early": School disengagement and exclusion among young people experiencing homelessness. In P. Towl & S. A. Hemphill (Eds.), *Safe, supportive, and inclusive learning environments for young people in crisis and trauma* (pp. 57–68). Routledge.

Henry, M., Cortes, A., & Morris, S. (2013). *The 2013 annual homeless assessment report (AHAR) to Congress, Part 1: Point-in-time estimates of homelessness.* U.S. Department of Housing and Urban Development, Office of Community Planning and Development. https://www.huduser.gov/portal/sites/default/files/pdf/2013-AHAR-Part-1.pdf

Henry, M., de Sousa, T., Roddey, C., Gayen, S., & Bednar, T. J. (2021). *The 2020 annual homeless assessment report (AHAR) to Congress, Part 1: Point-in-time estimates of homelessness.* U.S. Department of Housing and Urban Development, Office of Community Planning and Development. https://www.huduser.gov/portal/sites/default/files/pdf/2020-AHAR-Part-1.pdf

Hess, F. M. (1998). *Spinning wheels: The politics of urban school reform.* Brookings Institution Press.

Hopper, E. K., Bassuk, E. L., & Olivet, J. (2010). Shelter from the storm: Trauma-informed care in homeless service settings. *The Open Health Services and Policy Journal, 3,* 80–100.

Indiana Department of Education. (2011). *Education of homeless children and youth self-assessment guide.*

Ingram, E. S., Bridgeland, J. M., Reed, B., & Atwell, M. (2016). *Hidden in plain sight: Homeless students in America's public schools.* Civic Enterprises and Hart Research Associates. https://files.eric.ed.gov/fulltext/ED572753.pdf

Institute for Children, Poverty & Homelessness. (2016). *Aftershocks: The lasting impact of homelessness on student achievement.* Author. https://www.icph.org/reports/aftershocks-the-lasting-impact-of-homelessness-on-student-achievement/

Institute for Children, Poverty & Homelessness. (2024). *Homeless students in special education.* https://www.icph.org/specialed/

Jones, D. P., & Paulson, K. (2001). *Some next steps for states: A follow-up to "Measuring Up 2000."* National Center for Public Policy and Higher Education. https://files.eric.ed.gov/fulltext/ED475726.pdf

Kaysen, R. (2024, Jan. 25). More renters than ever before are burdened by the rent they pay. *The New York Times.* https://www.nytimes.com/2024/01/25/realestate/rent-prices-housing.html

Kezar, A., Hallett, R. E., Perez, R. J., & Kitchen, J. A. (2024). Scaling success for low-income, first-generation, and racially minoritized students through a culture of ecological validation. *Journal of Diversity in Higher Education, 17*(2), 229–242.

Kitchen, J. A., Perez, R. J., Hallett, R. E., Kezar, A., & Reason, R. (2021). Ecological Validation Model of Student Success: A new student support model for low-income, first-generation, and racially minoritized students. *Journal of College Student Development,* 62(6), 627–642.

Koschoreck, J. W. (2003). Accountability and educational equity in the transformation of an urban district. In L. Skrla & J. J. Scheurich (Eds.), *Educational equity and accountability: Paradigms, policies, and politics* (pp. 155–174). Routledge.

Kull, M. A., Morton, M. H., Patel, S., Curry, S., & Carreon, E. (2019). *Missed opportunities: Education among youth and young adults experiencing homelessness in America* [Brief]. Chapin Hall at the University of Chicago. https://www.chapinhall.org/wp-content/uploads/Chapin-Hall_VoYC_Education-One-Pager.pdf

Leithwood, K. (2010). Characteristics of school districts that are exceptionally effective in closing the achievement gap. *Leadership and Policy in Schools, 9*(3), *245–291.*

Levin, S., Espinoza, D., & Griffith, M. (2023). *Supporting students experiencing homelessness: District approaches to supports and funding* [Brief]. Learning Policy Institute. https://learningpolicyinstitute.org/product/supporting-students-homelessness-brief

Low, J. A., Hallett, R. E., & Mo, E. (2017). Doubled-up homeless: Comparing educational outcomes to low-income students. *Education & Urban Society, 49*(9), 795–813. https://doi.org/10.1177/0013124516659525

McKenzie-Mohr, S., Coates, J., & McLeod, H. (2011). Responding to the needs of youth who are homeless: Calling for politicized trauma-informed intervention. *Children and Youth Services Review, 34*, 136–143.

Merscham, C., Van Leeuwen, J. M., & McGuire, M. (2009). Mental health and substance abuse indicators among homeless youth in Denver, Colorado. *Child Welfare, 88*(2), 93–110.

Milburn, N. G., Stein, J. A., Lopez, S. A., Hilberg, A. M., Veprinsky, A., Arnold, E. M., Desmond, K. A., Branson, K., Lee, A., Bath, E., Amani, B., & Comulada, W. S. (2017). Trauma, family factors and the mental health of homeless adolescents. *Journal of Child & Adolescent Trauma, 12*(1), 37–47. https://doi.org/10.1007/s40653-017-0157-9

Miller, P. M. (2011). Homeless families' education networks: An examination of access and mobilization. *Educational Administration Quarterly, 47*, 543–581.

Miller, P. M., Pavlakis, A., Samartino, L., & Bourgeois, A. (2015). Brokering educational opportunities for students and their families. *International Journal of Qualitative Studies in Education, 28*(6), 730–749.

Miller, P. M., Wills, N., & Scanlan, M. (2013). Educational leadership on the social frontier: Developing promise neighborhoods in urban and tribal settings. *Educational Administration Quarterly, 49*(4), 543–575.

Milner, H. R., Murray, I. E., Farinda, A. A. & Delale-O'Connor, L. (2015). Outside of school matters: What we need to know in urban environments. *Equity & Excellence in Education, 48*(4) 529–548. https://doi.org/10.1080/10665684.2015.1085798

Morton, M. H., & Horwitz, B. (2019). *Research to impact: Federal actions to prevent & end youth homelessness.* Chapin Hall at the University of Chicago. https://www.chapinhall.org/wp-content/uploads/Federal-actions-to-prevent-and-end-youth-homelessness-final.pdf

Murphy, J., & Tobin, K. (2011). *Homelessness comes to school.* Corwin.

National Alliance to End Homelessness. (2020). *Fewer than 4 in 10 families with shelter stay have dedicated permanent housing support to exit homelessness.* Author. https://endhomelessness.org/resources/sharable-graphics/fewer-than-4-in-10-families-with-a-shelter-stay-have-dedicated-permanent-housing-support-to-exit-homelessness/

National Association for the Education of Homeless Children and Youth. (2013). *College access and success for students experiencing homelessness: A toolkit for educators and service providers.*

National Association for the Education of Homeless Children and Youth. (2016, April). *Summary of major amendments on homelessness and foster care in "The Every Student Succeeds Act of 2015".* http://www.naehcy.org/sites/default/files/dl/legis/ESEAFINALSUMMARYSHORTFINAL.pdf

National Center for Education Statistics. (2024). *Concentration of public school students eligible for free or reduced-price lunch: Condition of education.* U.S. Department of Education, Institute of Education Sciences. https://nces.ed.gov/programs/coe/indicator/clb

National Center for Homeless Education. (2021). *Federal data summary school years 2016–2017 through 2018–2019: Education for homeless children and youth.* Author. https://nche.ed.gov/wp-content/uploads/2021/04/Federal-Data-Summary-SY-16.17-to-18.19-Final.pdf

National Center for Homeless Education. (2022). *Graduation rates of students who experienced homelessness in America: School years 2017–2018 to 2018–2019.* Author. https://nche.ed.gov/wp-content/uploads/2022/09/ACGR-of-Students-Who-Experienced-Homelessness-in-America.pdf

National Center for Homeless Education. (2023). *Student homelessness in America: School years 2019–20 to 2021–22.* Author. https://nche.ed.gov/student-homelessness-in-america-school-years-2019-2020-to-2021-2022/

National Center for Homeless Education. (2024). *National overview.* https://profiles.nche.seiservices.com/ConsolidatedStateProfile.aspx

National Center on Early Childhood Health and Wellness. (2024). *Caring for the health and wellness of children experiencing homelessness.* Early Childhood National Centers. https://headstart.gov/sites/default/files/pdf/homelessness-tip-sheet.pdf

National Resource Network. (2015). *Hidden in plain sight: Why California's economically challenged cities matter.*

New York Equity Coalition. (2017). *Improving opportunity and achievement for students experiencing homelessness: Recommendations for New York's implementation of the Every Student Succeeds Act (ESSA).* Author. https://equityinedny.edtrust.org/wp-content/uploads/sites/6/2017/12/ESSA-Homeless-Brief_DIGITAL.pdf

Nichols, N. (2014). *Youth work: An institutional ethnography of youth homelessness.* Toronto University Press.

Obradovic, J., Long, J. D., Cutuli, J. J., Chan, C., Hinz, E., Heistad, D., & Masten, A. S. (2009). Academic achievement of homeless and highly mobile children in an urban school district: Longitudinal evidence on risk, growth and resilience. *Development and Psychopathology, 21*, 493–518.

Ohio Department of Education. (n.d.). *Partnering with families of highly mobile and homeless students.* https://education.ohio.gov/getattachment/Topics/Other-Resources/Family-and-Community-Engagement/Framework-for-Building-Partnerships-Among-Schools/Homeless.pdf.aspx

Pavlakis, A. E. (2015). Reaching all families: Family, school, and community partnerships amid homelessness and high mobility in an urban district. *Urban Education, 53*(8), 1043–1073. https://doi.org/10.1177/0042085915613547

Pavlakis, A. E. (2018). Spaces, places, and policies: Contextualizing student homelessness. *Educational Researcher, 47*(2), 134–141.

Payne, Y. A. (2017). Participatory Action Research (PAR). In B. S. Turner (Ed.), *Wiley Blackwell Encyclopedia of Social Theory.* John Wiley & Sons. https://doi.org/10.1002/9781118430873.est0272

Perlman, S., Sheller, S., Hudson, K. M., & Wilson, C. L. (2014). Parenting in the face of homelessness. In M. E. Haskett, B. A. Cowan, & S. Perlman (Eds.), *Supporting families experiencing homelessness: Current practices and future directions* (pp. 57–77). Springer.

Porter, A. C. (2005). Prospects for school reform and closing the achievement gap. In C. A. Dwyer (Ed.), *Measurement and research in the accountability era* (pp. 59–98). Routledge.

Portwood, S. G., Shears, J. K., Nelson, E. B., & Thomas, M. L. (2015). Examining the impact of family services on homeless children. *Child and Family Social Work, 20*(4), 480–493. https://doi.org/10.1111/cfs.12097

Powers, C. B., & Allaman, E. (December 17, 2013). *How participatory action research can promote social change and help youth development*. Kinder and Braver World Project, Born This Way Foundation & The Berkman Center for Internet & Society. http://cyber.law.harvard.edu/sites/cyber.law.harvard.edu/files/KBWParticipatoryActionResearch2012.pdf

The Road Map Project. (2015). *2013–2014 Regional Technical Report*. Community Center for Education Results. https://roadmapproject.org/wp-content/uploads/2018/09/Road-Map-Project-2015-Results-Report.pdf

Ronfeldt, M., Loeb, S., & Wyckoff, J. (2013). How teacher turnover harms student achievement. *American Educational Research Journal, 50*(1), 4–36.

Rorrer, A. K., Skrla, L., & Scheurich, J. J. (2008). Districts as institutional actors in school reform. *Educational Administration Quarterly, 44*(3), 307–357.

Samuels, C. A. (2007, June 19). Texas district makes gains with spec. ed. *Education Week, 26*(42), 34–37. http://www.edweek.org/ew/articles/2007/06/20/42speced.h26.html

SchoolHouse Connection. (2020). *Early childhood homelessness: An overview.* Author. https://schoolhouseconnection.org/article/young-children-experiencing-homelessness-an-overview

SchoolHouse Connection. (2024). *Overlooked and almost out of time: Pandemic-era funds for children and youth experiencing homelessness.* https://schoolhouseconnection.org/article/overlooked-and-almost-out-of-time-pandemic-era-funds-for-children-and-youth-experiencing-homelessness

SchoolHouse Connection. (2025). *The education of children and youth experiencing homelessness: Current trends, challenges, and needs.*.https://schoolhouseconnection.org/article/2025-fact-sheet-educating-children-and-youth-experiencing-homelessness

Sebring, P. B., & Bryk, A. S. (2000). *Leadership and the bottom line in Chicago.* Consortium on Chicago School Research. https://consortium.uchicago.edu/sites/default/files/2018-10/SchoolLeadershipAndTheBottomLine.pdf

Skobba, K., Meyers, D., & Tiller, L. (2018). Getting by and getting ahead: Social capital and transition to college among homeless and foster youth. *Children and Youth Services Review, 94*, 198–206.

Skrla, L., McKenzie, K. B., & Scheurich, J. J. (2009). *Using equity audits to create equitable and excellent schools.* Corwin Press.

Skrla, L., & Scheurich, J. J. (2003). *Educational equity and accountability: Paradigms, policies, and politics*. Routledge.

Southern Education Foundation (2015). *A new majority: Low-income students now a majority in the nation's public schools* [Research bulletin]. Author. https://southerneducation.org/publications/newmajorityresearchbulletin/

Spillane, J. P., & Diamond, J. D. (2006). *Distributed leadership in practice.* Teachers College Press.

Steele, W., & Malchiodi, C. A. (2012). *Trauma-informed practices with children and adolescents.* Routledge.

Taliep, N., & Ismail, G. (2023). Community mapping method. In P. Liamputtong (Ed.), *Handbook of social sciences and global public health* (pp. 823–844). Springer. https://doi.org/10.1007/978-3-031-25110-8_57

Tierney, W. G., Gupton, J. T., & Hallett, R. E. (2008). *Transition to adulthood for homeless adolescents.* Center for Higher Education Policy Analysis.

Tierney, W. G., & Hallett, R. E. (2012). Social capital and homeless youth: Influence of residential instability on college access. *Metropolitan Universities Journal, 22*(3), 46–62.

U.S. Census Bureau. (2021). *Current population survey: 2021 annual social and economic supplement.* Author. https://www2.census.gov/programs-surveys/cps/techdocs/cpsmar21.pdf

U.S. Department of Education. (2004). *Education for homeless children and youth act: Title VII-B of the McKinney-Vento Homeless Assistance Act: Non-regulatory guidance.* Author.

U.S. Department of Education. (2016). *Education for homeless children and youths: Non-regulatory guidance.* https://www.ed.gov/sites/ed/files/policy/elsec/leg/essa/160240ehcyguidance072716.pdf

U.S. Census Bureau. (2024). *Nearly half of renter households are cost-burdened, proportions differ by race* [Press release]. Author. https://www.census.gov/newsroom/press-releases/2024/renter-households-cost-burdened-race.html

Venegas, K. M., & Hallett, R. E. (2008). When a group presentation isn't enough: Financial aid advising for low-income urban college bound students. *College and University, 83*(4), 16–25.

Woelki, W. T., Hallett, R. E., & Aviles, A. M. (2025). *Increasing access to higher education for students experiencing homelessness: Utilizing transition plans to empower students.* Pullias Center for Higher Education at the University of Southern California. https://pullias.usc.edu/download/increasing-access-to-higher-education-for-students-experiencing-homelessness-utilizing-transition-plans-to-empower-students-brief/

Yosso, T. J. (2005). Whose culture has capital? A critical race theory discussion of community cultural wealth. *Race Ethnicity and Education, 8*(1), 69–91. https://doi.org/10.1080/1361332052000341006

Index

About the Authors

Ronald E. Hallett is a professor of education in the Rossier School of Education at the University of Southern California and a former public school teacher. With a focus on low-income student populations, his research examines the intersection of educational policies, educator practices, and student experiences. He has published extensively in peer-reviewed journals as well as co-authoring six books. He consistently engages in practice-oriented research that explores topics such as college access, homelessness, and systemic barriers in education. His work has influenced educators, policymakers, and community leaders, promoting meaningful change in education systems.

Ann M. Aviles is an associate professor in the Department of Human Development and Family Sciences at the University of Delaware. Her research areas include examining policies, services, and programs that impact the educational opportunities, material realities, and mental health of youth experiencing homelessness/instability, and positive youth/community development. Dr. Aviles is the author of a book and numerous peer-reviewed articles that explore how schools can leverage community partnerships to support students, including those who are homeless and housing-insecure. Dr. Aviles has worked with several community-based organizations to encourage educational access for students experiencing homelessness.

Linda Skrla is a professor emerita at Texas A&M University. A former public school teacher and administrator, her research focuses on school and district leadership, including accountability policy, high-success school districts, and women superintendents. She is a past vice president of Division A of the American Educational Research Association (AERA), former editor of *Educational Administration Quarterly*, and coauthor or coeditor of several books that explore promising practices for educational leaders to leverage to improve student experiences and outcomes. Dr. Skrla has collaborated with numerous schools and districts to adjust policies and practices to improve student experiences and outcomes.